Hunters in the Wilderness

Opening and Closing the Frontier

by

Michael R. Weisser

in collaboration with

William A. Weisser

**Volume 2 of 4 Volumes:
Guns in America**

Published by:

TeeTee Press
Ware MA 01082

Cover design by Damonza

ISBN: 0615943357
ISBN-13: 978-0615943350

10 9 8 7 6 5 4 3 2 1

First Edition

To the memory of Herman Smotiler, who knew me better than anyone else.

FOREWORD / AUTHOR'S NOTE

This book, like all the books in this series, is an attempt to introduce a perspective into discussions about guns that is based on facts seen through the lens of my personal experiences. It is not an argument either for or against guns and it is certainly not an effort to promote a certain point of view about the ownership or use of guns. It is based on a great deal of published scholarship, cited in the 'Further Reading' section that follows the text, plus some primary research that I have done both in printed and digital collections, along with interviews and first-hand conversations. And that's all it is. Not an attack, not a defense, just a book.

AUTHOR'S OTHER BOOKS

The Peasants of the Montes: Roots of Revolution in Spain

Crime and Punishment in Early Modern Europe

A Brotherhood of Memory: Jewish Landsmanshaftn in the New World

Guns for Good Guys, Guns for Bad Guys: Gun Violence in America

CONTENTS

CHAPTER 1

WHAT IS WILDERNESS?

In August, 1968, I was eating breakfast in a diner in Buffalo, Wyoming, deciding whether to drive up and through the Big Horn Mountain Range that loomed just ahead. I wanted to reach Worland, stay there overnight, and then get to the Tetons and Yellowstone the next day. As I went to pay my bill at the counter, I noticed everyone spinning around on their stools to look out the front window and a quick glance in that direction alerted me to the fact that it was starting to rain like hell. I paused to drop a tip on the counter and the waitress, who could tell I was passing through, asked me whether I was driving into the mountains to which I nodded a "yes."

And she said, "Maybe you want to sit here and wait for the rain to end because up there it'll be a lot of snow."

"'Up there' meant the Ten Sleep Canyon that I was going to take to get through the Big Horn

1

Range. But what did this waitress from Buffalo, Wyoming know about snow that I, a graduate student from New York now living in Chicago, didn't know about snow? For that matter, what did she know about anything that I didn't know at least twice as much?

So out I went, driving west on Route 16 through a fierce rainstorm whose huge droplets battered my windshield as my car drove straight up a long, steep hill and entered the Big Horn Range. Twenty minutes later I was sitting in my car somewhere inside Ten Sleep Canyon, the rain had turned into a blizzard and I was dead stuck in a drift that obliterated even the slightest outline of the road. The good news was that I had filled the tank in Buffalo, the bad news was that I had a compact car with a tank that only held about seven gallons of gas. Was there enough fuel in the tank to keep the engine running so that neither I nor the car would freeze? I wasn't sure.

There were no cell phones in 1968. There was nobody waiting for me in the towns ahead who would put out the alarm if I didn't show up. I hadn't hiked into the backwoods and gotten lost, I hadn't been climbing a wall of the canyon and slipped down. I was sitting in my car on a well-paved, two-lane state highway at 11 o'clock in the morning and if something lucky didn't happen there was a good chance I was going to die. Obviously something lucky did happen, and what happened was that at some point late in the afternoon, when the gas gauge was beginning to indicate that I was truly in a bad way, a huge snowplow came lumbering up behind me, swerved around and slowly cleared the road for me all the way through the canyon and down to the point where the snow once again turned into rain.

That was 1968. Now let's drop back a bit to 1876. On July 1st, a reporter from Chicago's Herald Tribune named John Finerty is with General George Crook and a small group of staff officers on a hunting trip into the Wind River Range. Crook was in Wyoming to settle the Indian business once and for all. Things had been more or less quiet until 1874 when a young military colonel named George Armstrong Custer did the first survey of the Black Hills in South Dakota and reported the existence of gold.

Between prospectors whose claims had dried up in California and entrepreneurs and adventure-seekers from back East, the ensuing human wave that flooded onto the Great Plains quickly brought an end to Indian control of the territory and, more important, Indian hunting practices and living conditions. Because until the gold rush into the Black Hills, the few whites who came west to live on the plains were essentially hunters and gatherers, different from the natives in that they left their families far behind, but similar in that they only used natural resources that needed to be consumed in order to survive.

Precisely because permanent white settlement on the frontier was initially so sparse and transient–whites weren't *conquering* the wilderness, only living in it–the initial government reaction to the demands of Indians to retain suzerainty over their landscape was met with accommodation and a general willingness to allow things to continue as they had. This attitude was reflected in the Fort Laramie treaties signed by more than 30 Sioux chiefs (including Sitting Bull) in 1868, which guaranteed perpetual ownership of the Black Hills and other territories and uncontested settlement of most of what is now the north-western part of Nebraska, the western half of South Dakota and the eastern half of Wyoming, altogether some 50,000 square miles. In return for total control of this territory, which included the dismantling of military installations, the natives agreed to give non-natives free passage through their lands, as well as to respect the right-of-way of the railroads, whose first coast-to-coast line was just about to be completed.

On paper the natives got the better deal. On paper. In reality, the agreements were meaningless and within six months after they were signed, disputes leading to armed conflicts broke out, which eventually turned into the Great Sioux War of which the most famous battle was the massacre of General Custer and his 7th Cavalry unit on a hillside above the Little Bighorn River. The battle, payback time for Custer's 1867 slaughter of the Cheyenne at Washita River, took place on June 26, 1876, and was as yet unknown by General Crook or John Finerty as they hunted through the Big Horn Range on July 1st.

Taylor's Ridge at Big Horn Range from the west

Crook and his unit wouldn't hear about the Custer debacle for another ten days, most of which were spent hunting and exploring through the Big Horn Range. As near as I can figure out, the detachment set up a base camp about 20 miles north of where I got stuck in Ten Sleep Canyon, and according to Finerty, it was he and Crook's aide-de-camp Colonel Mills, who went out on a hunt and ended up crossing from the east to the west side of the Bighorn Range. Finerty described the area as follows:

> "We passed lake after lake and stream after stream. The trees increased in size and variety, and the vegetation assumed a tropical richness. Dozens of American eagles rose majestically from the rocks and soared proudly above us...."

Golden's Creek looking east from Bighorn Range – taken by the author.

Finerty believed, and perhaps he was correct, that he and Mills were the first two white men to actually cross from the eastern to the western slopes of the Big Horn Range. They did it on foot, having left their mounts somewhere behind. But they were hardly the first humans to have made that difficult trip. In fact, Crook's column followed a trail used by the Snake Indians which, according to Finerty, went through somewhat inaccessible country because the Snake hunters always wanted to steer clear of the Sioux. In fact, Crook had hired more than 30 Indian scouts to guide his column from Laramie up to the region where he expected to engage the Sioux, because his maps simply couldn't be used to show him the way.

Why so many scouts to cover a trek of less than 300 miles? Because each scout knew a little piece of the landscape but none could vouch for knowing how to traverse the entire route. This was no different from the experience of the first military column to travel through the Great Plains and Rocky Mountains, the Lewis and Clark expedition that set out to cross the Louisiana Purchase in 1804. Attention has focused for the most part on the female Shoshone guide, Sacagawea, whose knowledge of trails through the Rockies were to that expedition what the Ten Sleep snow plow was to me, but the expedition encountered more than 30 different tribes and utilized endless local natives to help guide them overland and navigate rivers and streams.

The easterners whose moving and then settling westward brought about the opening and closing of the American frontier in less than a century had a mind-set that was a product of Old World experiences and traditions. And chief among this mind-set as it relates to the theme of this book was the idea that the process of building a nation had absolutely nothing to do with either conquering a wilderness or closing a frontier. In a confidential letter written by Thomas Jefferson to Congress that accompanied his request for funds to cover the costs of the Lewis and Clark Expedition, the President noted that the Louisiana Purchase threw open the possibility that a vast amount of land would now be open to settlement but would require a willingness on the part of the Indians to "abandon hunting" and thus share the resources of their land with white farmers.

The fact that native inhabitants of the North American wilderness were decidedly un-Christian in their religious and cultural beliefs only enhanced the whole notion of wilderness as an untamed and unsettled place, because going back to the Old Testament one could find specific reference to such events as Adam and Eve being expelled from Eden or the Hebrews wandering for 40 years as examples of the degree to which wilderness was considered an unholy place out of which people escaped *into* civilized, settled communities. It was therefore not in the interest of modern societies to preserve wilderness, or even really think about it, but rather to quickly explore it, tame it and exploit it.

But the remarkable thing about the American frontier, as opposed to frontiers that had previously existed in all other western societies, was that our frontier still existed long after our version of civilization had reached and settled the eastern and western shores. In Europe, the word 'frontier' had long ago ceased to denote an unsettled place. Rather, for at least a thousand years if not longer, it was used to define a political boundary between civilized, settled national states. To all extents and purposes, the European continent was entirely rid of a physical wilderness by the time that Charlemagne was crowned Holy Roman Emperor in 800 AD. It would be nearly another eight centuries before a native living on what would become the North American continent would actually encounter a white westerner face to face.

It is not clear when the actual wilderness disappeared in Western Europe, but by the time Caesar led the Roman legions through Germany and into Gaul during the 1st Century BC, he encountered sizable numbers of indigenous populations, and considered himself to be leading a military conquest to extend Roman control over what was already settled lands. And even though the Romans referred to the indigenous populations of Germania and Gaul as "savages," this did not reflect any judgment that these tribes were living in a wilderness zone. The Roman conquest of non-Mediterranean Europe, which was the last time that unknown territory was opened to Western exploration and exploitation until Columbus set sail, represented an organized effort by an organized society to extend its political domain, rather than an incursion into an unsettled "wilderness" zone.

The history of frontier and wilderness versus settlement and civilization in the United States was entirely different. From the moment that Europeans landed on the eastern shore, they encountered indigenous populations, and while there was continued but sporadic resistance to the development of coastal cities, interior farmlands and the creation of formal, political boundaries and jurisdictions, white settlers did not consider the East Coast or its hinterland to be a wilderness zone, and for every Indian tribe that mounted active resistance to the incursions of Europeans, there was another tribe that found themselves engaged in trade and mercantile relations with the White populations.

The recognition that America would be extending its settlement into a true wilderness began to develop, albeit briefly, after the Louisiana Purchase in 1803, and the first, formal attempt to explore and chart the contours of this huge, new territory with the Lewis and Clarke expedition in 1804. By 1831, as Alexis de Tocqueville made his celebrated trip across America, he journeyed through the as-yet untouched forests in the Michigan territory but still remarked on how quickly the frontier was being transformed into a settled and civilized society. Although the settlers living on the edge or within these forests barely possessed the most minimal accoutrements of civilized existence (scraps of clothing, rudimentary furnishings inside of small, shabby dwellings, etc.) de Tocqueville noted that everyone he met seemed busily trying to sell enough goods and raise enough money to create a "copy" of the civilized society they had left behind.

When white Americans began moving across the continent to settle the Oregon and Washington territories in the decades before and after the Civil War, there was little consideration given to doing much about the wilderness zone that lay between the two coasts. And even when the indigenous populations began resisting the infiltration and transient occupation of their native lands, the U.S. government reacted in tepid fits and starts until the point was reached when complaints about lack of security for travelers and tradesmen forced the national government back in Washington to intervene.

Little by little, the indigenous populations that inhabited the territory that lay between the Missouri River to the east and the Rocky Mountains to the west began to understand that the continued (and increasing) presence of white transients and settlers would ultimately bring about a life-or-death confrontation between these two civilizations. I don't use the term 'civilization' loosely or for reasons of political correctness to describe the indigenous populations of what we now call the Great Plains. I use the term because the first whites to encounter this population–

white hunters–understood that they were dealing with their equals, if not their betters. But more on that issue below.

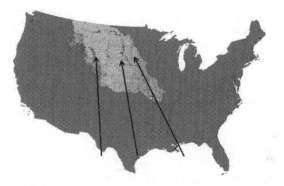

Rocky Mountains, Great Plains and Missouri River

Ultimately, the battle between Indians and whites was a battle over the control of land. And I make this point because even though "taming" the wilderness was one of the results of the victory of whites over Indians, it was incidental to the main thrust of the conflict itself. The reason for the conflict was not that there was such a competition for land between the two civilizations, nor was land a resource that was in short supply. In 1870, when the major battles over the great Plains started to break out, the white population of North and South Dakota, Wyoming, Montana and Idaho was under 60,000, the indigenous Plains population about the same number, or a little more. Add in 10,000 soldiers and government agents, and the entire population of the Great Plains was less than half the number of people then living in Chicago.

So the conflict known as the Indian Wars didn't break out because the frontier was getting crowded. It broke out because two competing civilizations viewed and used the natural resources of the frontier zone differently, chief among those resources being land. Recall that I previously mentioned the 1868 treaty that allegedly secured nearly the entire Great Plains for indigenous populations in perpetuity. This treaty was followed, three years later, by an Act of Congress that prohibited more treaties or compacts between the United States of America and any indigenous population because the latter could not be considered sovereign nations with whom the United States could conduct business. In other words, from our perspective, Indians didn't have a government.

[Note that I am speaking here of the Plains Indians. In fact, a recent discovery of early Indian governance documents by the Library of Congress shows that many of the eastern tribes, like the Cherokee, had formal, even written Constitutions that set forth the legal relationships and described government hierarchies within and between the various tribal groupings, some of these documents dating from well before the American Constitution was produced.]

The reason that Indian tribes didn't have governments the way we had a government was because the Indians had no need of laws in the way that we had and used laws. And the reason that Indians didn't have laws was exactly the reverse of why we *did* have laws; namely, to allocate and control the use of land. One of the Old World practices that we used in taming our wilderness first appeared in England after the Norman Conquest, and it involved the development of the Common Law to settle disputes over land. The whole point of legal procedure was to mitigate land disputes so that feuds between competing claimants to land could be eliminated or controlled, and it was the traditions and practices of Common Law that stood behind the development of constitutional government, first in England and later in the colonies.

The development of government, first in the Old World and then carried over to the New, rested on the notion that some kind of sovereign power would fairly arbitrate disputes between individuals, families, clans, or whatever type of personal relationships were used to differentiate between contesting parties. While the type and manner of designating sovereignty evolved over time from single, hereditary leaders to representative bodies elected by popular mandate, the notion of government as Western societies understood and practiced it assumed a hierarchy of power and authority in which decisions arrived at by the political leadership were adhered to by all the stakeholders to that issue, as well as by everyone who considered themselves to be members of the polity that acknowledged the authority and sovereignty of a particular political hierarchy.

Most of the indigenous populations that lived in what whites called the 'wilderness' had no concept of hierarchical authority, nor did they necessarily have to respect the decisions made by tribal chiefs in their name. The 30-odd chiefs who put their marks on the 1868 agreement at Fort Laramie were speaking only for themselves and these chiefs could not enforce their decision to make peace with whites when they returned and spoke about the treaty with their tribes. When warriors from some of these tribes refused to accept the treaty's terms and continued to attack whites who were coming across the Plains, this was not in any way behavior that was out of character with the traditions and social relations within a tribe. As Francis Parkman said about the tribe that he visited outside of Fort Laramie: "In this democratic community, the chief never assumes superior state."

The indigenous populations of the Great Plains and other parts of the frontier could not base their behavior on our notions of property ownership for the simple reason that they were not permanently settled on specific chunks of land. They were transient, they moved from place to place as the seasons changed and herds looked for fresh food, and they occupied but did not own land. This different use of the primary wilderness resource was explicitly recognized in the letter that President Thomas Jefferson sent to the Congress that requested funding for the Lewis and Clarke expedition in 1804. By "encouraging" Indians to abandon hunting, according to Jefferson, "the extensive forests necessary in the hunting life will then become useless," and more land could be thrown open to white settlement in the newly-acquired domains.

But encouraging Indians to stop hunting was different from preventing them from hunting by forcing them to move about only within a delimited space and eliminating the game which was the point of the hunt. It's usually thought that the Buffalo, for example, was only found on the Great Plains, but in fact until 1800 they were also native to the East. Why did they disappear from parts of Pennsylvania and rural New York by the beginning of the nineteenth century? Because they were all hunted and trapped or shot, a practice that continued and increased further west as travel and settlement of whites began to occur from coast to coast.

Buffalo were the most recognized but hardly the only game species that indigenous populations used for food whose herds were thinned or made close to extinct by the behavior of whites. As early as the 1840's, such important game as wild turkeys and white-tail deer were already disappearing in eastern areas where they had been important resources for the indigenous populations of those regions. In fact, colonial archives contain laws limiting hunting of various species from as early as the 1660's. The disappearance of game animals was an immediate result of wilderness settlement, particularly when an animal, such as the buffalo, became an article of commercial value for the urban marketplace.

Indigenous populations were aware of the competitive threat posed by white settlers from the moment the two civilizations encountered one another. Sometimes the encounter was peaceful, other times it led to disputes and war. But once white America realized that the wilderness held resources that could either be exploited by settling people within the frontier zone, or extracting and moving natural and commercial resources out of the frontier zone, the treatment of the indigenous populations became just another normal and expected step in the transformation from wilderness to civilization.

Except what we considered wilderness was already civilized. Why do I say that? Because every bit of the territory that lay between the two coastal regions was occupied by civilized populations, regardless of whether or not we considered them to be civilized. Again, I'm not saying this to be politically correct. I am saying it for the simple reason that, as far as I can tell, the indigenous populations that inhabited what whites considered to be wilderness met the criteria that we apply to the definition of civilization, namely, an organized society based on recognized values, roles, language, culture and history. Every Indian tribe encountered by Lewis and Clarke, for example, met this criteria and, more important, distinguished themselves from all other tribes on the same basis.

See a great difference between the two family groups? I don't, and neither did the earliest whites who first started coming into contact with the Indian populations in what was considered the wilderness frontier. Here's an excerpt from the diary kept by Jedediah Smith during his exploration of California in 1826:

> The country through which we travelled was quite rough and mountainous. I found at that place about 35 lodges some of Skins and some of

Brush. Each family has 4 or 5 horses. These Indians are constantly moving about like the snakes [considered to be the most warlike tribe] and at this time live almost entirely on Service Berries which are now ripe. I found these Indians more honest than any I had ever been with in the country. They appear to have very little disposition to steal and ask for nothing unless it may be a little meat. As stealing and Begging are the most degrading features in the Indian character and as their prevalence is almost universal so to be exempt from then is no ordinary merit. The Ute's are cleanly quiet and active and make a nearer approach to civilized life than any Indians I have seen in the Interior. Their leggings and shirts which are made of the skins of the Deer Mt Sheep or Antelope are kept quite clean.

Smith, who was born in a town outside of Albany, NY, went west in the 1820s to hunt and trap furs, an enterprise that enlisted the energies of most of the early wilderness explorers. In 1824 he crossed the Sierra into California, which was then Mexican territory, and later journeyed up the

California coast to become the first white American to enter the Oregon territory. He extensively explored and mapped the Rocky Mountains and discovered the South Pass, which was the point at the Continental Divide that was then used for all of the pioneers moving both to California and Oregon. Even though I was more than one hundred miles east and north of South pass, I thought about Smith while I was sitting in my car and wondering if I would survive the blizzard in Ten Sleep Canyon.

South Pass, Wyoming

Most of the mountain-men who crisscrossed the western frontier were unable to read or write, not surprising in a society in which literacy was still the privilege of a few. But enough early travel accounts were written and have survived to give us a fairly coherent picture of Indian life and, what is more, the degree to which the indigenous populations that we encountered exhibited all of the traits of civilization that I enumerated above. Here's a commentary by Nathaniel Wyeth, who led two expeditions to Oregon in 1832 and again in 1834, specifically his description of an Indian fishing activity that he witnessed in 1832:

> In morning went to see the Indians catch Salmon which is done by entangling them in their passage up the creek among dams which they erect and spearing them they catch an immense quantity the operation commences in the morning at a signal given by their chief. This chief is a good sized man and very intelligent and the president would do well if he could preserve the respect of his subjects as well or maintain as much dignity.

The President referred to by Wyeth at the time of this expedition was Andrew Jackson.

Another view of Indian behavior can be found in the diary of John Kirk Townsend, who was attached to the 1834 Wyeth expedition and described a visit by a band of Snake Indians, who were usually considered to be more warlike and less 'civilized' than many of the other western tribes:

> The Indians remained with us until dark, and then left us quietly for their own camp. There are two lodges of them, in all

about twenty persons, but none of them presumed to come near us, with the exception of the three men, two squaws, and a few children. The chief is a man about fifty years of age, tall, and dignified looking, with large, strong aqualine features. His manners were cordial and agreeable, perhaps remarkably so, and he exhibited very little of that stoical indifference to surrounding objects which is so characteristic of an Indian.

Finally, note the comments by Thomas James who first went west in 1810, but shared his views on Indians in the 1840s. By the latter date, James lamented the degree to which the Indian population was physically decimated by contact with whites, in particular, as a result of the alcohol trade. This was particularly upsetting because he could recall character and behavioral traits that marked the Indians, particularly their leaders, as people of great distinction. To quote:

I have seen some of the finest specimens of men among our North American Indians. I have seen Chiefs with the dignity of real Princes and the eloquence of real orators, and *Braves* with the valor of the ancient Spartans. Their manner of speaking is extremely dignified and energetic. They gesticulate with infinite grace, freedom and animation. Their words flow deliberately, conveying their ideas with great force and vividness of expression, deep into the hearts of their hearers. Among their speakers I recognized all the essentials in manner of consummate orators.

The comments by James and Townsend, the appearance of the word 'dignity' in describing the behavior of Indian leaders, should not be discounted as just a figure of speech. The men who first went west in the pay of commercial merchants and traders were a rough-hewn bunch, usually lacking in anything but the most basic life skills. They knew how to hunt, they knew how to survive in desolate surroundings, but the fact that they were *white* did not make them cultured or civilized beyond the most rudimentary state. One might wonder, in fact, whether the actual level of civilization regressed among the Indians after they encountered whites. Because the hunters brought things into Indian society, like infections and alcohol, which could only result in a rending of civilized relations that the Indians were powerless to prevent.

The best estimates of the size of the indigenous population throughout the continental United States in 1850 puts the total at around 700,000. Fifty years later, the total probably was around 535,000, but most of these were found in the Southwest and the Eastern coastal states. In the region between the Missouri and the eastern slope of the Rockies along with the Oregon-Washington Coast, the loss was at least half, and this largely demographic catastrophe occurred in a period of roughly thirty years. This was also the period when a bison herd that had numbered in the millions was reduced to a few thousand roaming around in Yellowstone Park.

How could a population that was decimated so completely and suddenly not have exhibited a complete and total breakdown of the social relationships that defined and measured the ways in which they lived? And yet we find again and again that white hunters who went into the wilderness learned from the indigenous peoples, depended on them and frequently ended up living with or amongst them. Here's another diary from a member of the 1832 Wyeth expedition named John Ball:

Mr. Frapp had an Indian wife who traveled along with him, and the Indians of the party, some of them, had their wives, these women as good horsemen as the men, always riding astride. One day we delayed our march, we knew not why, till after a time we heard an outcry for a few minutes from Frapp's wife, out to one side in some bushes. And we soon learned the cause of our laying over, was to give her the opportunity to lay in, give birth to a child in camp and not on our day's march. But the very next day, she sat her newborn baby, feet down, into a deep basket that she hung to the pummel of her saddle, mounted her horse and rode on in the band as usual. And she had another child of two or three, who had his own horse. He was sat on the saddle and blankets brought around him so as to keep him erect, and his gentle pony went loose with the other pack horses, which kept along with those riding and never strayed from the common band. I mention these things to show something of the Indian ways in their own country, and that whites in their country readily

> from necessity and convenience, fall into
> like habits, and soon find but little
> inconvenience from the same.

The whites, it is noted, fall into "like habits, and soon find but little inconvenience from the same." Of course the white hunters and explorers copied the habits of the Indians. How else could they have survived? After all, what they had learned in the space occupied by their own civilization gave them little, if any preparation for going out on the frontier and figuring out how to live in this great unknown.

How different were the attitudes towards indigenous populations that were expressed by residents of the settled zones of America, most of whom who had no concerns about wilderness beyond the fact that it needed to be opened and exploited as quickly as possible. In fact, most whites considered the wilderness to be a harsh, unyielding and, most of all, the antithesis of civilized life. In fact, it was assumed that the further that people went into the wilderness, the more they shed civilized behavior and became one with the pre-civilized environment. This view was expressed best by the President of Yale University, Timothy Dwight, who stated that the further people pushed in to the wilderness, the

more they became "less and less a civilized man."
And this wasn't written by Dwight on the dawn
of western discovery; it appeared in 1822, the
same time that these "less-civilized" men were
already crossing the Rocky Mountains and
mapping the Continental Divide.

Oregon Trail

It took only twenty years for the wilderness
zone explored by hunters and trappers to become
a well-traversed route across the continent known
as the Oregon Trail. And in just thirty years, from
1839 to 1870, more than a half million settlers,
homesteaders and plain travelers moved along all
or part of this great roadway west. And the
promoters of the trail, particularly the commercial
interests who wanted the Oregon territory to be
settled as quickly as possible, never stopped
reminding the pioneers that the trials and travails
of their journeys imbued them with a sense of the
importance of their task. As Roderick Frazier
Nash put it in his masterful study, *Wilderness and*

the American Mind, "the conquest of wilderness bolstered the national ego."

Precisely because the wilderness, by definition, was a wild and "unclaimed" place, this also meant that its bounties and resources could be exploited simply by going *out there*, claiming whatever of value could be found, and bringing it to market where it could be traded or sold. The hunters who went into the wilderness in the 1820s to gather furs weren't constrained by laws, property rights or anything else. And it was the Indians, the permanent residents of the so-called wilderness, who showed them where to hunt, how to cross the mountains, what was needed in order to survive.

But the moment that these hunters came together to trade furs and arrange shipments back east, then this is where one civilization began to challenge the other. Because even though most of the early mountain-men lived just like the indigenous populations that they met in the mountains, and many lived not only like the Indians but within Indian society and tribes, they didn't come to this territory in order to live out their lives by taking what they needed in order to survive. They weren't hunting as part of the natural cycle of birth, growth, death and decay which allowed nature to replenish and restock the natural zones. They took what they could out of the territory because what they hunted and killed was worth a bounty back home.

We often think that the difference between white and Indian social development is reflected in the comparative technologies employed by the two populations: whites had the railroad, Indians didn't even know the wheel. But the real difference between us and the people we encountered when we pushed back the frontier can best be understood with reference to an event that took place once each year in the Wyoming territory known as the fur trade rendezvous, where fur traders met each other and their eastern suppliers to transact the trade and commerce of furs.

Fur trade rendezvous on the Green River

This encampment took place for the first time in 1825 and for the last time in 1840. Beaver pelts had been coming out of the West even prior to the Louisiana Purchase, but once the territory east of the Continental Divide was owned by the United States, explorers and trappers began to develop the fur industry on an organized basis. By the 1820's there were numerous trappers working on or near the many tributaries that flowed from the Rockies down to the Missouri and Platte Rivers, many of whom were either customers or contractors for major trading companies, including the Hudson Bay Company and the American-Pacific Fur Company owned by Jacob Astor.

The fur trade rendezvous took place at various sites along the Green River near South Pass in Wyoming, as well as once in Utah and once on the western side of the Tetons, near what is presently the Idaho town of Driggs. These annual meetings, which were no different from modern trade shows like the COMDEX electronics show in Las Vegas, may have grown out of tribal trade fairs held on the Green River which attracted Shoshones, Utes, Crows, Flatheads and Nez Perce tribes. And even though Indians continued to participate in the fur trade rendezvous until these trade fairs ended with the collapse of the international fur trade after 1840, there was one crucial difference between Indian and white events, namely, the white fur traders operated as modern entrepreneurs in every sense of the word; the Indians, on the other hand, engaged in barter as their medium of exchange.

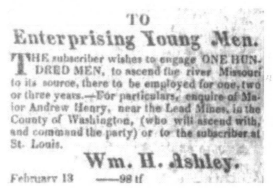

Advertisement in St. Louis newspaper for trappers to work for the Henry-Ashley Company

The above advertisement was run as a classified ad in St. Louis newspapers by the Henry-Ashley Company in 1822. It was William Ashley's decision to build a large fur-trading enterprise which led to the development of the rendezvous system, because using one centralized location to supply trappers with needed goods in return for their pelts was an efficient and cost-effective way to manage the trade.

Ashley's ability to understand and organize a commercial venture that operated over thousands of square miles was not unlike the mentality of other entrepreneurs who would transform the American west from a wilderness to an enterprise zone. The United States was the only country in the entire world that ever industrialized and conquered a frontier at the same time. By the time the mountain-men began showing settlers how to travel through the wilderness, we had already dug thousands of miles of canals and were starting to lay railroad track from coast to coast. Large cities were developing in territories where mountains still remained to be mapped, factories were finishing and shipping goods around the world using raw products that had first derived from the Indian trade.

Conquering the wilderness didn't impede the growth of civilization; it enhanced the growth of civilization because the inexhaustible supply of products and resources from the wilderness were made available at a very cheap price. And the reason why the land and everything on it cost so little to secure? Because the populations that lived in what we called wilderness didn't put a price on what we took away. Which is why we called it a frontier or a wilderness. If what we meant by those words was a place where civilized people didn't live, then by the time the mountain-men went west from the Missouri River, or even earlier when Boone crossed the Appalachians through Wilderness Gap, the wilderness had long ceased to exist. But even if it didn't exist, we could always invent it again. And in the present-day argument over hunting and conservation, we keep inventing it again and again.

Chapter 2

Enter the Gentleman Hunter

Theodore Roosevelt was born into wealth and privilege. As a result, he was able to make decisions about his life and career that did not impinge on either his desire or his need to earn a living. He could, in effect, blend his interests with his vocation, and his interests from an early age revolved around nature, animals and land.

Roosevelt came by his love of nature and natural things honestly. His uncle, Robert B.

Roosevelt, also known as RBR, was an avid fisherman and naturalist, who in 1858 published a critically-acclaimed work, *Game Fish of the Northern States of America, and British Provinces*, which excited readers on both sides of the Atlantic. Not only was this book a critical success, but it also placed the Roosevelt family and name in the forefront of the newly-emerging conservation movement. In *Game Fish* and a second work published in 1865, Robert Roosevelt began to proselytize for environmental regulation of fishing zones because he had already noticed the dearth of game fish in the Hudson River and other waterways adjacent to New York.

Meanwhile, TR's father, Theodore Roosevelt, Sr., was himself just as engaged in the protection of natural things, serving as a founder and trustee of the Museum of Natural History, which would eventually become the storehouse for thousands of animal, bird, flora and fauna specimens that his son would collect over the years. By the time Teddy Roosevelt was a teenager, with the encouragement and often participation of his father, he had hiked throughout much of the lower Hudson Valley, expeditions that were then extended into the Adirondacks, the mountain ranges of New Hampshire and Maine, and the fishing zones of the Long island Sound, in particular near the family's summer retreat in Oyster Bay.

Roosevelt's first real encounter with wilderness took place in 1880 when, just short of his 22nd birthday, he and his older brother Elliott embarked on a series of extensive hunting and travel trips using Chicago as their home base. Let's bear in mind that this trip took place just four years after Custer and his 7th Cavalry were slaughtered at the Little Big Horn, and while the scene of that massacre lay one thousand miles west of Chicago, much of the territory between Lake Michigan and the Great Plains was still largely unknown, if not unmapped. The National Geological Survey had just been formed the previous year, and although most of the Midwest states had already come into the Union, none of the territory north of the 40th Parallel (the line of the transcontinental railroad) between the Missouri and the Pacific was yet either settled or claimed. Of the 1.2 billion acres in this region still belonging to the Federal Government, it was estimated that maps existed for less than one-fifth of the landscape.

In all, TR and Elliott made three hunting trips away from Chicago to rural Illinois, Iowa and

Minnesota, in the last trip getting to the border of the Dakotas. They were accompanied by a guide named Wilcox, whose Illinois farm was also a rest stop during what Douglas Brinkley calls this "tramp" through the Midwest, and their guide also hired additional manpower to help along the way. As the expedition moved further and further from Chicago they shot more grouse, met fewer people and basically witnessed the edge of the wilderness being turned into settled territory.

While both TR and his brother affected the dress and mannerisms of frontier life, they didn't for a moment lose their Eastern patrician moorings. In a letter to his sister Corinne, TR commented that "our fare and accommodations are of the roughest," and in the middle of the trip took time out to send his sister Anna a very detailed letter containing a list of all the clothing that she needed to have ready for him on his return to New York: "my afternoon suit, 2 changes of underflannels, 6 shirts, 6 pr. silk socks, handkerchiefs, neckties, 2 pairs of low shoes, razors, and my beaver hat." In the middle of nowhere, the young frontiersman Roosevelt could remember that he didn't want to be without his silk socks.

Roosevelt didn't return to the West for three years. In the interim he married, travelled through Europe, went to Law School, served in the New York State Assembly and purchased a home on West 45th Street in New York. He busied himself with numerous civic organizations and projects, as members of the monied class tended to do, along with designing and building a summer home on Long island that would be known as Sagamore Hill, and would serve as the Summer White House from 1902 to 1908. He also spent time decorating both the city and country homes with trophies of animals taken on various hunts, and it was his desire to add a buffalo head to the trophy room in the Manhattan brownstone that sent him out to the West again. By the early 1880s what was left of the North American bison herd, which had at one time been native from coast to coast, had been reduced to a tiny fraction of its former size, for the most part found only in the Dakotas and several other, more remote parts of the northern Great Plains. The disappearance of the buffalo herd was, normal assumptions to the contrary, not because the transcontinental railroad had cut the bison's natural migration path in half. Rather, it was the ability of the railroad to bring buffalo skins out to the market and tourist-hunters in to shoot more of the animals that depleted almost the entire stock in less than twenty years. A herd that was estimated to number forty million in 1860 had dwindled to perhaps less than several thousand by the 1880's. Roosevelt's desire to bring back a trophy head in 1883 was prompted by the knowledge that if he waited much longer, there wouldn't be a single trophy to be found.

The hunting expedition to find and kill a buffalo took place in September and lasted for fifteen days. On several occasions Roosevelt shot and either wounded or completely missed a trophy, or followed creeks and eddies up and down throughout the North Dakota Badlands without even seeing a bull. Finally, he bagged a nice buffalo on a day that took him for the first time into the Montana territory, and with the trophy head wrapped in burlap, took a Pullman sleeper back to New York. While making preparations for the hunt Roosevelt also purchased the first of two ranching properties located to the south and north of the town of Medora in on the edge of the North Dakota Badlands; the area surrounding the Little Missouri River that lies between the two properties is now Theodore Roosevelt National Park.

Theodore Roosevelt NP – courtesy of Sean Palfrey to whom I
owe many thanks.

I'll skip over Roosevelt's experiences as a cattle rancher because, suffice it to say, the venture was hardly a success. The reader can get details on this and other aspects of Roosevelt's Western experience either by reading Douglas Brinkley's remarkable book, *The Wilderness Warrior*, or accessing the Roosevelt website maintained by Dickinson State University. More to the point, upon Roosevelt's return to the East with his trophy bison head, he followed the legacies of his father and uncle and plunged into a commitment and activism about nature that lasted for the remainder of his life. Chief among these activities as they relate to the theme of this book was his friendship and collaboration with George Bird Grinnell and the founding of the Boone and Crockett Club, which placed hunters like himself

in the forefront of conserving wilderness habitat and frontier.

Like Roosevelt, George Bird Grinnell was also born to privilege, and after growing up on the grounds of the Audubon estate in upper Manhattan (and being educated by Audubon's widow) Grinnell attended Yale University where he became enamored with nature, ended up earning a Ph.D. in zoology and decided to devote himself full-time to the study of wildlife and natural environments. He first went to the West as part of the Custer expedition to the Black Hills in 1874 and wisely declined Custer's invitation to accompany him on the trip that culminated with the Little Big Horn massacre in 1876.

The same year that Custer's 7th Cavalry column met up with the combined forces of Gall, Crazy Horse and Sitting Bull, Grinnell became editor of a national magazine, *Forest and Stream*, which along with other national publications like *American Sportsman* and *Field and Stream* (the latter merged with *Forest and Stream* in 1930) began to define and champion the sporting, as opposed to commercial approach to hunting and fishing. Readers of these publications, as John Reiger has so aptly written, "looked upon themselves as members of a fraternity with a well-defined code of conduct and thinking." This meant, among other things, practicing "proper etiquette in the field," giving game a "sporting chance," and going out on a hunt as much to appreciate the aesthetics of nature as to come home with the kill. In other words, hunting as a gentlemanly pursuit.

George Bird Grinnell

Even though Grinnell and Roosevelt's friendship got off to a rocky start when Grinnell wrote a negative and somewhat sarcastic review of Roosevelt's book *Hunting Trips of a Ranchman*, sooner or later the two would have found each other and made common cause. Not only did they both purchase Western ranches in 1884, Roosevelt in North Dakota, Grinnell in Montana, but they moved in the same social circles and defined their interests in nature and wilderness exactly the same way. And they were both hunters, a shared passion that led them to co-found the Boone and Crockett Club in 1888.

If one wanted to construct a list of America's social elite at the end of the nineteenth century, the B&C membership list could serve as a start. Want a few names? Try Eastman, Galbreath, Mellon, Morgan, Olin, Rockefeller and, of course, Roosevelt. It wasn't very difficult for Roosevelt to populate the early membership list of Boone & Crockett, because all he had to do was contact the board members of New York's Museum of Natural History which, as I mentioned earlier, was basically founded by TR's father.

Boone & Crockett was launched, in fact, as part of the effort by Roosevelt, Grinnell and others to create America's first real natural preserve, Yellowstone Park. The park had been established by law in 1872, but it took more than 20 years of arguing, persuading, lobbying and agitating before this remarkable space was finally set aside and protected once and for all. In the process of creating and defining the park's mission and goals, the entire concept of a national park system began to develop and ultimately came into being in 1916. Not by accident, one of the Park Service's first Directors, Horace Albright, was also an early joiner of the B&C. In addition to the Yellowstone campaign and the later emergence of the national parks, Boone & Crockett was also in the forefront of efforts to establish the National Forest and National Wildlife Refuge systems, programs which embody the club's commitment (as stated in its founding charter) to "promote the conservation and management of wildlife, especially big game, and its habitat, to preserve and encourage hunting and to maintain the highest ethical standards of fair chase and sportsmanship in North America."

In addition to promoting the idea of saving natural habitat, Roosevelt also used B&C to promote himself. By lobbying federal officials for the protection of Yellowstone and other natural preserves, Roosevelt was able to inject himself onto the national stage and remind influential business and civic leaders that he was available for public service. In 1888 he was appointed to the Civil Service Commission and was then named Assistant Secretary of the Navy in 1897. He resigned from this position and ended up achieving real national stature by leading the Rough Riders up San Juan Hill in 1898, a series of cavalry charges that actually ended with Roosevelt walking up the hill because his horse couldn't negotiate the final climb.

Campaigning strongly for McKinley in the 1900 election, Roosevelt took the oath as Vice President at the beginning of McKinley's term, only to become President when McKinley succumbed to the wounds from his assassination on September 14, 1901. I don't need to add additional details about Roosevelt's life in and out of politics following his accession to the office of the Presidency, because more has been written by and about him than certainly any other American of his time. But it should be noted that in his seven and one-half years as Chief Executive, his achievements in the area of conservation and natural preservation were immense. Through the creation of parks, nature preserves and national forests (nearly the entire state of Idaho was set aside as protected forest), he is credited with conserving or at least managing more than 225 million acres of land, and his friendships with leaders of the conservation movement like Gifford Pinchot, John Muir and George Bird Grinnell proved to be of vital importance to the growth of conservation and environmentalism in the century following his death.

But to understand how Roosevelt's views shaped the American debate on frontier and wilderness, we have to go back to the time when he first encountered wilderness himself, which was in the years following his purchase of the North Dakota properties in 1884 and his own, nearly three-year residence on those ranches while recovering from the untimely deaths of his mother and his first wife. It was during this stay in North Dakota, with frequent trips back to New York and elsewhere, that Roosevelt not only experienced the outdoors in a way that put the final stamp on his love and devotion of the natural environment, but also gave him the opportunity to hunt in ways not unlike the hunting activities of the early explorers and mountain-men who had preceded him on the frontier. These hunting episodes formed the basis of perhaps his two best books on the West, *Hunting Trips of a Ranchman*, that was dedicated to his brother Elliott and published in 1885, and the shorter *The Wilderness Hunter*, which was finished at Sagamore Hill and published in 1892.

These two books, particularly *Wilderness Hunter*, replaced Francis Parkman's *The Oregon Trail* as the pre-eminent descriptive work of the American frontier. Parkman's book, published in 1847, gave easterners a view of the opening of the West that combined historical and personal narrative with first-hand accounts of the sights and landscapes that pioneers and settlers would encounter as they made the immense trip from the Mississippi port city of St. Louis to the Pacific Coast. Forty years later, when Roosevelt sat down to record his experiences hunting in the Dakotas and Wyoming, the Oregon Trail had been displaced by the transcontinental railroad and Parkman's version of the journey West no longer counted for anything but a memory of times past.

What made these books so popular was Roosevelt's ability to paint with text the most vivid descriptions of the western landscape which people back east were beginning to view through photographs that appeared in mass-circulation magazines and other books. Here's a brief description of a sunset from *Hunting Trips of a Ranchman*: "...the sun had set behind a row of jagged buttes, that loomed up in sharp relief against the western sky; above them it had left a bar of yellow light, which only made more intense the darkness of the surrounding heavens." And even though Roosevelt took some literary liberties with his descriptions of various game animals (which George Bird Grinnell pointed out in rather critical terms before they became fast friends), his genuine love and devotion to the singular beauty of the Great West and its wildlife fascinated the public that bought and read his books.

By the time Roosevelt published these popular works, however, he was keenly aware that the frontier of which he was so enamored had come to an end. And just as the wilderness had disappeared, so had the wilderness hunters whose activities and history were what attracted TR to live and hunt on the Great Plains. As he noted in the first chapter of *The Wilderness Hunter*: "The frontier had come to an end; it had vanished. With it vanished the old race of wilderness hunters, the men who spent all their days in the lonely wilds." But Roosevelt also understood the vital role these early hunters had played in the exploration and opening of western lands, for "in every work of exploration…the adventurous hunters played the leading part."

Much of the success of these books lay in the degree to which Roosevelt was able to bring the spirit and style of these wilderness hunters to life in the descriptions of his own hunting experiences. But there was something else of importance in what the early hunters and trappers did for shaping the history and development of the country, namely, they were the advance troops for the great wave of civilization that washed across the wilderness with the appearance of white settlers, ranchers and travelers. To quote Roosevelt again in *The Wilderness Hunter*: "Boone and his fellow-hunters were the heralds of the oncoming civilization, the pioneers in that conquest of the wilderness which has at last been practically achieved in our own day."

What is captured in that passage (and so many others) is the degree to which Roosevelt's admiration of the early explorer-hunters was tied to his belief that they were engaged in the all-important task of spreading civilization into places that previously were wilderness and, therefore, uncivilized. And what about the other population that inhabited the wilderness zone? TR's views of the Indians is best caught in passages from his four-volume *The Winning of the West*, published between 1889 and 1896, which set out clearly the extent to which the conflict was between people who did not own the land, as opposed to people for whom land ownership was the fuel that charged the engine of economic growth.

Not only did the land claims made by Indians conflict with any modern conception of property, according to Roosevelt, had the government honored such claims it would have had to honor similarly spurious claims made by some of the early explorers, hunters, trappers and miners who often settled or exploited land that they didn't truly own. "With the best intentions," notes Roosevelt, "it was wholly impossible for any government to evolve order out of such chaos without resort to the ultimate arbitrator – the sword." Of course Roosevelt lays aside the question of who won and who lost when the sword was brought out to arbitrate the issue of land ownership once and for all. And he also neglects to mention that many of those self-same explorers and wilderness hunters found it convenient and financially worthwhile to stop hunting animals and start hunting Indians when the military looked to purchase their knowledge of the frontier zone.

But we shouldn't be so quick to judge Roosevelt harshly on these issues given that, from his perspective, the conflict between white Americans and red indigenous peoples was really no more than a sideshow to the much greater issue of the day, namely, the necessity to open up the vast territory—more than one-third of the entire land mass of the continental United States—whose resources would generate an extraordinary cycle of economic growth. Recall the list of personages—Galbreath, Mellon, Morgan et al.—who graced the early Boone & Crockett membership list. They and many other eastern magnates made their fortunes through developing the financial and material infrastructure that unalterably transformed the West. One of Roosevelt's best friends and another inaugural Boone & Crockett member was the great grand-nephew of none other than William Astor, whose fur traders described in the previous chapter first made easterners aware of the natural bounties that could be extracted from the frontier. One could hardly fault Theodore Roosevelt for clinging to ideas that sprang naturally from his background and social class.

Thus, from the beginning of the modern conservation movement, Roosevelt and the other conservation advocates tried to find a way to balance the needs to preserve habitat with the demands of economic growth that increasingly relied on the exploitation of resources from what had previously been the wilderness zone. The strategy employed by the conservationists took two forms: on the one hand, curbing excessive hunting through the establishment of seasons, limits and other regulations that sought to keep balance between species survival and game kills; on the other hand, setting aside natural environments in which species could flourish and herds and flocks continue to grow.

The first piece of land that was ever set aside as a wildlife refuge was a three-acre island off the east coast of Florida near Vero Beach known as Pelican Island. The legislation was signed into law by TR in 1903, and it protected the nesting site of both the brown pelican and other exotic water birds whose feathers, also known as plumes, were in great demand for expensive fashion-wear in New York and other centers of the high-end clothing trade. This law was followed in 1905 by a more general statute that created the mechanism for setting aside land as wildlife refuges throughout the United States.

Notwithstanding the ultimate purposes of these laws, which was to protect endangered species by giving them an immunity from destruction at the hands of hunters, the creation of wildlife refuges also reflected a time-honored tradition of the elite classes which from earliest times considered the development and ownership of private hunting preserves to be an important mark of upper-class gentility and status. By the second half of the eighteenth century, upper-class sportsmen banded together to purchase and manage vast tracts of land in undeveloped regions of the Adirondacks and eastern Pennsylvania, where limiting the number of people who could gain access to the territory meant, by definition, that wild species would be protected in these zones.

But the major effort by the sporting classes to preserve habitat took the form of rationalizing and developing state and local laws that controlled hunting on both public and private lands, laws which, as John Reiger has pointed out, initially took the form of encouraging the destruction of species by paying bounties for killing animals whose existence threatened livestock and crops. The disappearance of the bounty system and its replacement by codified regulations that set seasons and limits was not without its critics, in particular non-hunting farmers who often hired commercial hunters to rid their farms of predators that otherwise would endanger their animals and fields. And while growing urban populations were increasingly dependent upon commercially-developed foodstuffs for the everyday diet, there were still plenty of communities, particularly in poorer, less-developed rural areas, who consumed meat supplied by local, commercial hunters who sold at prices well below the costs of market food. I lived in South Carolina in the mid-70s and I was told by the head of the state wildlife authority that game meat represented as much as 40% of all the meat consumed in Colleton and other low-country counties. This was told to me in the 1970's, not the 1870's.

It was left to George Bird Grinnell to come up with a rationale for strict hunting laws that would reflect the conservationist ethos while at the same time allow the non-elite to pursue hunting for more utilitarian purposes. After all, he said in an editorial in *Forest and Stream* in 1881, it was people without large incomes who would benefit most from game laws because "the rich man can travel to distant fields where game is plenty, and can have his shooting whether the laws are enforced or not. With the poor man it is not so; he has to take his day or half day when he can get it, and has neither the time nor money to travel far in search of game."

Grinnell's use of laws and government authority to make hunting a "democratic" exercise would be a hallmark of Theodore Roosevelt's Progressive political philosophy, which sought to use government regulation to bring the greatest good to the greatest number of people, not just in terms of hunting, but in all social and economic affairs. But the problem with this message. and Grinnell's conception of the democratization of hunting through government liberalism, was that when Roosevelt went hunting in the Dakotas and Wyoming, and then wrote best-selling books about his experiences, he wasn't behaving like a "gentleman" of the upper class who could afford to travel to "distant parts," far beyond the authority of government laws and regulations. If anything, he pretended to be another wilderness explorer who was attracted to the uncharted domains because a man could "live and hunt on his own." The mountain-men and trappers who came together at the Green River Fur Trade Rendezvous each year were able to earn large sums for their hunting precisely because they operated in areas far beyond government constraints. And if the trappers made money from their endeavors, the entrepreneurs back east for whom they worked made much more. When John Jacob Astor died in 1848 he was probably the wealthiest person in the United

States. And even though his investments in New York real estate increased his wealth enormously, his fortune really came from his near-monopoly of the Great Lakes fur trade in earlier years. So while Progressives and elitists like Roosevelt and Grinnell might have believed that hunting regulations could be developed that would level the playing field and allow for hunting and conservation to exist side by side, the truth is that the financial rewards from commercial hunting were most evident in areas where government didn't exist at all.

What ended commercial hunting on the frontier was not the extension and activity of government. What ended it were the technologies of supply and production that became the hallmarks of the Industrial Revolution. Even though, as I mentioned earlier, as late as the 1970's there were still places in the Southeast where game meat was a dietary staple, most Americans by the beginning of the twentieth century were consuming store-bought foods. It was the development of refrigerated railroad cars and warehouses that ended cattle drives from Texas up across the Plains. And it was the enormous increase in beef consumption that produced mountains of leather cattle hides as a substitute for hides from the buffalo which had all been hunted and destroyed. As we will see in Chapter 3, it was the Industrial Revolution that differentiated between people in the cities and people on the farm, and it was the Industrial Revolution that created a vast, urban market for products whose value had initially sent explorers and hunters out to the frontier.

In addition to the resources from the frontier that fueled the economic growth of America, there was also an important cultural, indeed ideological legacy spawned by the closing if the frontier. This was the notion of American "exceptionalism" that was found in all of Roosevelt's western writings and was based upon the idea that no other country had conquered such a vast territory so quickly and, in the process, created a nation and national identity unlike any other. The shaping of a unique American character because of the frontier experience then became the watchword of American historians, as exemplified by Frederick Jackson Turner's "classic" essay of 1893 which described how the Westward expansion, in the words of William Cronon, "reinvented direct democratic institutions, and reinfused themselves with an independence and a creativity that was the source of American democracy and national character."

Turner's essay, which borrowed heavily from a speech delivered by Roosevelt six months earlier to the Wisconsin State Historical Society, was also originally delivered as a speech in Chicago, an event that coincided with the great 1893 World's Fair. The fair not only marked Chicago's complete recovery from the devastating fire that had leveled most of the city after Mrs. O'Leary's cow kicked over the lantern in 1871, but was a celebration of the extent to which the United States was moving towards occupying the premier position in the world economy, given the unprecedented growth in technology and manufacturing over the previous fifty years. In fact Roosevelt actually had a hand in one of the exhibits, but in his case it wasn't something that showcased the "miracle" of electricity or the machine-engines that produced all sorts of assembly-line items. Rather, it was a rustic log cabin in which were displayed relics that had belonged to the very first mountain-man and hunter, Daniel Boone, along with other old hunting and trapping equipment that had been lying around Roosevelt's ranch. The cabin was sponsored by the Boone & Crockett Club because Roosevelt and the other club members were anxious to show visitors what they believed were the *true* circumstances that existed on the frontier; a region and an historical epoch whose achievements then allowed the country to celebrate its world prominence at the Chicago Fair.

But stimulating a love of country is one thing, building a country is quite another. The role and activities of hunters ultimately became part of a great legend that celebrated the taming of the frontier as a fundamental contribution to the development of the American character and the American ideal. What hunters really achieved was the initial exploitation of wilderness resources whose use would then take the American economy to remarkable heights. Roosevelt was able to sentimentalize the frontier because a century of economic growth allowed him to detach himself briefly from his eastern, upper-class moorings created by that growth and travel through the West developing his portraits of a wilderness that had long since disappeared. He was also able to bring into question the use of hunting to exploit wilderness resources because by the time 'gentleman hunters' like himself went on wildlife shoots, we had developed much more efficient methods to extract needed materials from the frontier. Which is what the next chapter is all about.

CHAPTER 3

WILDERNESS GROWS THE ECONOMY

I drove across the country for the first time in 1975. Because we had two drivers, myself and my brother, we drove each day from sun-up to sundown and made it from coast to coast in five and one-half days. We took the fastest and most direct route and since it was December, drove most of the way along a southerly route through Kentucky, Tennessee, Arkansas, Oklahoma, the desert states of New Mexico, Arizona and then into Southern California. On the way we picked up pieces of Interstate 20, the majority of the miles not yet complete. Ten years later I drove the same route again, the interstate was finished and the trip took just slightly more than four days.

What impressed me about the trip both times was that as I drove west, the space between every point of human existence got wider, the cities and towns got smaller, the conditions of the highways got better and the vehicles moved faster. This gradual diminution in the degree of human existence became noticeable after we crossed the Mississippi and got less and less until we were about forty miles from Los Angeles at which point it was as if I was back on the East Coast.

The vast, uninhabited spaces of the American continent from the 91st Meridian – the Mississippi – until the 121st Meridian – the eastern slope of the Sierras – was really no different in 1980 than it had been in 1880 or 1780. The census of 1800 set the total U.S. population at 5,300,000, but counted people only living in twenty states and territories, of which none, with the exception of something called the Northwest Territories that contained 45,000 people, lay farther west than the Mississippi River.

A century later, the 1900 census set the total population at almost 63 million, of whom 35 million occupied what was considered the entire United States territory a century earlier, with the other 28 million now found in places that hadn't even been part of the country at the end of the nineteenth century. But more than the growth in the country's expanse was the growth of the economy. Contemplate the following estimates of country-by-country GDP:

	1820	1870	1913
USA	12,548	98,374	517,383
UK	36,232	100,180	224,618
Germany	22,535	41,814	95,487
France	35,468	72,100	144,489
Italy	22,535	41,814	95,487
World	694,598	1,110,951	2,733,365

In millions of 1990-adjusted (PPP) dollars.

From the beginning to the middle of the nineteenth century, every advanced country except the US more than doubled its economic output. Our economy grew by a factor of five. But note what happened from 1870 to the year preceding World War I (and it was 1914-1918 that our economy really expanded due to trade with Allied countries.) The other advanced economies again doubled in size but the US economy grew at even a faster rate than in the previous period. In 1870 the US economy represented about 10% of the world's economic output; it grew to one-fifth of the world's economy over the next four decades

The growth in GDP can also be seen with reference to population growth. In 1820, the population of the United States was 9,600,000, of whom 1.5 million were slaves. The total US population, including slaves, represented exactly

10% of the population of the other industrialized countries, which together numbered 96 million inhabitants. By 1870 the US population was about 20% of the industrialized world, and by 1910 about one-third. This population growth, particularly the emergence of large, urban populations, is what fostered the extraordinary development of an internal market, with the consequent increase in national and per capita GDP.

Where did all these people go to live? In 1800, nearly the entire US population inhabited the original 13 colonies, which of the total US population of 53 million, more than 47 million were resident within the Eastern seaboard states. Add in Georgia and the District of Columbia and the Atlantic population was more than 90% of the country as a whole. Remember that this was three years prior to the Louisiana Purchase, so if there were Americans living west of the Mississippi they wouldn't have been counted at all. Nor did we count the Indians, either west or east of the Mississippi. But they had their chance in Chapter 1, remember?

The geographic demography of the United States changed dramatically in the decades following the Louisiana Purchase, which tells us where all those people went who were counted as living in the United States over the remainder of the nineteenth century. By 1870, with a total population of nearly 63 million, only 27 million were in the original seaboard states, with 18 million now residents of the upper Midwest (Michigan, Iowa, Illinois, Missouri, Minnesota, Kansas, Idaho) and 3 million more living on the Great Plains. The Southwest and West Coast populations were also more than 10 million, but many had been there prior to 1800 when these territories were still part of Mexico and thus couldn't be included in any population count of the United States.

The point to be made is that when we talk about the American wilderness, we usually are talking about the vast expanse of territory between the Mississippi River on the one hand, and the western edge of the Great Basin on the other. The mountain men who went through South Pass in the decades immediately following the Louisiana Purchase didn't cross a political frontier unless they chose to go into California where the Henry Expedition ended up in 1822, much to the anger of the Mexican authorities who threatened to arrest and lock them all up. So what we referred to as 'the frontier' was something that in Europe had a much different meaning, because their wilderness had disappeared more than one thousand years before virtually any white Americans even possessed a map that showed them how to travel through our western zones.

But it didn't take very long for all of this to change. By the 1850's the upper Midwest was completely settled, by the 1870's the railroad ran coast to coast and trunk lines were being built, and by 1890 the U.S. Census declared the frontier to be "closed." It can't just be coincidence that the extraordinary expansion of the American economy over the second half of the nineteenth century took place at the very same time that the American wilderness was settled and disappeared.

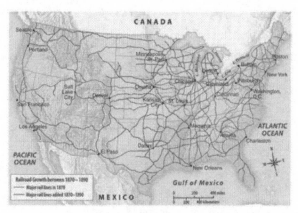

Railroad lines in 1870 (green) and 1890 (red)

In the two decades between 1870 and 1890, every state and every territory in the United States was pierced by rail lines. And this picture is far from complete, because it only shows major "trunk" lines, not the hundreds of smaller, "spur" lines linking smaller communities, silos and cattle pens with the major lines which then brought products to and from national market hubs. In the 1820's it took two weeks to journey from New York to Chicago. Seventy years later, Teddy Roosevelt could travel from his ranch in North Dakota to his townhouse in Manhattan in less than five days, during which time he could sit in his Pullman car and write about hunting in the wilderness (sic) around his ranch.

But it wasn't so much the speed at which resources from undeveloped zones got to the market, it was the cost. Because just as Europe had used up its wilderness centuries before the New World was even explored, the relative lack of basic resources like wood and coal in other industrial zones contrasted with their abundance in the American environment. And the more abundant basic products were, the cheaper their cost and the greater margin and profits that would accrue to everyone involved in the production of market goods.

Take, for example, the development of coal mining and coal-fired industry. By the beginning of the nineteenth century, coal was being used primarily to power transportation steam engines, but increasingly it was used for factory production and, by the end of the nineteenth century, to run electric turbines. The total production of coal in the four most industrialized European countries at the end of the nineteenth century was roughly 390 million tons; coal production in the United States alone was almost equal to that number. If you were a factory-owner in France or Italy you had to import coal from England and Germany which meant competing for a badly-needed resource with home-grown enterprises in Germany or the UK. American coal consumers had to compete with one another for coal, but they didn't have to compete with anyone else.

The abundance of natural resources in the less-settled American frontier zones was even more pronounced when it came to a primary materials like wood. Because in the case of coal, Europeans did not extract it in great amounts prior to the Industrial Revolution, so it didn't matter that they had closed their wilderness many centuries prior to the Industrial Age. But wood had been a necessary resource for dwellings in Europe since the beginning of modern times.

Which meant, by definition, that most of the wood used to build homes and factories in Western Europe during the nineteenth century had to come in from abroad.

Where did it come from? Much of it came from the United States, with the port of Bangor Maine shipping nearly 9 billion board feet of timber between 1832 and 1888. Much of this resource went to other American cities, as well as to the Caribbean and various South American ports. But all of this trade simply meant that entrepreneurs in the United States could draw a double benefit from the abundance of this natural product, once again a function of the existence of a vast frontier zone. It also meant settlement in areas near the frontier could take place at a very fast rate, because there were no limits on how many homes and other buildings could be constructed at a relatively cheap cost. The best example of this is Chicago, which grew in size from 30,000 in 1850 to more than one million in 1890, a startling growth unmatched by any other major city over the same period. New York, for example, increased in size from 600,000 to 2.3 million, while Philadelphia grew much more quickly, from 120,000 to just over one million, and St. Louis went from 77,000 to 450,000. These were all impressive developments, but no city's growth matched what took place on the shores of Lake Michigan.

It would be a mistake however, to assume that the growth of Chicago, St. Louis, Kansas City and other large metropolitan centers on the edge of what had been the frontier only reflected a one-way movement of resources from this vast wilderness hinterland to the urban markets and then beyond. The shift of resources from West to East of course played an important role in the growth of the national economy. But what is often overlooked in economic histories of the Gilded Age is the extent to which America's remarkable emergence as the pre-eminent economic power of the Western world was due, in large part, to the creation of a vast, internal market within what had been the frontier zone itself. This two-way exchange between city and countryside is best described by William Cronon, who describes Chicago during this period as "the busy hive" because of the degree to which the city acted as a transfer point, organizing the "westward flow of merchandise" that was paid for by "the stream of natural resources moving in the opposite direction."

Let's take a more detailed look at how the geographic distribution of population changed in the decades following the Civil War. In 1850, the U.S. population stood at slightly more than 23 million, of which 22 million lived east of the Mississippi; in other words, within the county's borders as they existed at the time of the Louisiana Purchase. In 1900, the country's population stood at 76 million, of which roughly one-third lived within the Louisiana Purchase territory, the Southwest and the West Coast. Most of these settlers, more than 21 million, were settled in the Midwest farm belt and the Plains states. By comparison, neither England, France or Italy had a total population of 40 million, which meant that in 1900, what had been our wilderness fifty years previously now held half as many people as the entire national populations of the major industrialized countries in Europe.

But before we get further into the settlement of the Western frontier, let's back up a bit and take a look at the earlier stage of wilderness penetration that began to take place from the moment that the East Coast was the site of the Pilgrim community and other early presences of European whites. The fur trade that provoked the movement of hunters to the West after Lewis and

Clark was not a new development. In fact, it was an extension of the activity of hunters and trappers who began trading for beaver pelts with the Indians or taking furs themselves from the moment that white settlements appeared. Within ten years after the Plymouth landing in 1620, perhaps more than 100,000 beaver furs were shipped back to Europe, a number which may have increased to almost 100,000 each year for the decade ending in 1640.

It's not clear how much of this international trade was due to exchanges with the eastern Indians, but it was certainly a substantial part of the enterprise. The early European fur hunters, whether they operated in what was first French Canada or further south in the original British coastal colonies, could not have developed a fur trade in the New World without help from the indigenous populations in both regions. And it was the ability of Europeans to barter furs for items desired by the Indians, particularly firearms, ammunition and other metal-based implements, that gave local tribes the incentive to take European hunters into wilderness areas that contained beaver and other pelts, or transfer furs directly to Europeans themselves, or both.

The first guns that whites used to barter for pelts were manufactured in England, with the earliest record of such a transaction dating from 1623. Within two decades, the guns for pelts exchange had become so strong that the British Crown issued the following order in 1641: "In trucking or trading with the Indians no man shall give them for any commodity of theirs, silver or gold, or any weapons of war, either guns or gunpowder, nor sword, nor any other munition, which might come to be used against ourselves." The royal order was certainly a dead order by the time it reached the colonies, if not before, particularly because arms made and imported from England were soon supplanted by firearms manufactured in the colonies, in particular the long-barrel or Kentucky rifle, as it was known, that the mountain men carried with them into the eastern forests and beyond.

Wilderness hunters, in search of furs, soon found themselves moving over the Alleghenies and other eastern slopes and quickly pushed the frontier back to the Mississippi where it would remain until after the Louisiana Purchase in 1803. Furs had become critically scarce in the coastal regions due to incessant hunting on the one hand, and the clearing of woodland for planting on the other. The result of the depletion of beaver in this region also created a dramatic change in the ecosystem that beavers had created but where they no longer lived. By blockading and damming streams, beavers created watersheds of languid, slow-moving water that retained vast amounts of silt and gradually transformed marsh into fields and then forests. The picture below shows this transformation taking place today:

Picture by the author. New Salem, MA.

Remove the beaver away from his habitat and these flat, slow-moving streams quickly become sharp gullies with rushing water that, particularly after heavy rains, erodes banks, widens the channel and replaces ponds with cataracts. The picture below shows the remains of a retaining wall that was built perpendicular to a narrow but fast-moving creek (in the background) whose torrent provided the power for a local mill.

Picture by the author. Monroe Plateau, MA.

Wherever farmers opened forests to farmland, beavers were immediately extinguished, streams could power mills and, as population grew even larger, local mills could turn into factories. As hunters moved west to find and deplete more fur-bearing animals, in the east they left behind a new ecosystem that was the perfect infrastructure in which to launch the industrial age. Because what the early industrial revolution required above all was access to cheap, raw materials and the ability to harness abundant energy. Pushing the frontier westward meant the exploitation of raw materials like wood, furs and leather at a price that would never have been possible had these goods only been made available from a European market whose frontier had been closed for more than one thousand years. But remaking the original wilderness ecosystem in the east coupled these abundant raw materials together with an energy source that cost nothing at all.

For all the talk about how the explorers and early wilderness hunters chose to remove themselves from 'civilization' and live free from the constraints of settled life, the wilderness also offered immense economic potential precisely because it could furnish the raw materials that were increasingly utilized by the ever-advancing industrial engine that was developing alongside the wilderness in the developed zones. And what made these products so inviting was not only their abundance because the wilderness *had never previously been exploited as a reservoir for industrial growth*, but because the inhabitants of this wilderness, from the perspective of the hunters and explorers, didn't own these resources at all. Hence, the only cost involved in moving raw materials and raw foodstuffs from the frontier to the market were the costs of extraction and transportation. Rarely, if ever, did the hunters and explorers have to pay resource costs at all. In fact, while there were endless disputes between whites and Indians over land and hunting rights, the major conflicts that took place over who would reap the economic benefits of exploiting the wilderness took place between competing white nations themselves. The French and Indian War, for example, which resulted in the British laying claims to Canadian and northern American territories originally explored by the Spanish and the French, broke out because of competition for wilderness zones that were the natural hinterlands of British colonies first established on the East Coast.

The war, which lasted from 1754 to 1763, erupted over control of the Monongahela and Allegheny Rivers, which had become the primary means of transporting goods to and from areas east of the Allegheny Mountains (Pennsylvania and Ohio) to Canada and thence back to France. The French constructed a fort at the confluence of the two rivers, at what is now present-day Pittsburgh, and war broke out with the ambush of a French military force by a British column of Virginia volunteers led by our future first President. Washington, incidentally, was sent to Pennsylvania to help secure the commercial interests of the Ohio Company and other investors who were busily staking out economic zones of influence in this wilderness zone.

The conflict between competing trading companies from different countries ended in the east with the Revolutionary War and then the purchase of the Louisiana Territory in 1803 and the annexation of Florida from Spain in 1822. But the competition for wilderness resources then shifted westward as the scope of wilderness penetration expanded following Lewis & Clark. Here again, the fact that Indians were not "owners" of wilderness resources in the modern sense reduced the costs of raw materials from the frontier that continued to flow back to settled and manufacturing zones. And while the Plains Indians, like the Indians who had first encountered whites on the eastern coast, often reacted negatively to the presence of a population with whom they would have to share their settlement lands, the attempt by Indians to challenge white exploitation of the wilderness never involved questions of ownership, or the monetary value of what might be bought or sold.

Like the way in which beaver pelts attracted early wilderness hunters into the eastern forests and then beyond, so buffalo hides became a major commercial resource once hunters and explorers began to trek across the West following the example of Lewis and Clark. The bison had largely vanished east of the Missouri by the beginning of the nineteenth century; so, for that matter, had the beaver. Thus, when the Lewis and Clark expedition saw their first herds and were surprised that they numbered around five hundred, it was little more than astonishing when they then reached the Great Plains and encountered herds that were sometimes twenty-five miles wide.

Like the beaver, although perhaps not with the same degree of engineering skills, the bison's movements and habits also created a unique ecosystem that could not be replicated once the herds disappeared. The bison's grazing pattern tended to be not at all steady in terms of how the animals moved across the land, but rather, based on taking the vegetation completely from a specific grazing spot and then moving to another spot disconnected from the first. Hence, they tended to clear fields in disconnected patches which allowed grasses to replenish themselves much quicker and accelerate density and plant cover for other living things.

Alone among the animals that grazed on the plains, buffalo also engaged in 'wallowing,' or rolling around on open land, which created more compact soil and aided in water retention in areas where they moved. This made it easier for other forms of wildlife to find water, as well as aiding in biodiversity for the ecosystem as a whole. Bison were also, of course, a primary foodstuff not just for indigenous peoples, but for the many predatory animals that shared space with them in the plains, in particular grizzlies and wolves, although the latter tended to prefer elk. Even the animals have their gourmet standards. But the animals that subsisted partially from preying on the bison left the carcass behind, and as it decayed, it fed additional nutrients to the soils which created a richer biomass.

All of these ecological benefits disappeared when the buffalo, like the beaver before them, were hunted to near-extinction as the western wilderness was turned into a settled, civilized zone. But losing the buffalo meant that the land they formerly occupied could also become a resource for the development and growth back east of industrial zones. And in particular it meant that the vacant spaces left by the now-absent herds of buffalo could be utilized by farmers and cattlemen whose products helped satisfy urban demand for foodstuffs which, in turn, paid the costs of manufactured goods that flowed from the manufacturing centers back out to the rural zone. And it also meant that the costs of both the raw materials flowing east and the finished goods moving west did not have to reflect the value of the land which produced the raw materials on the one hand and utilized the finished products on the other. Because as long as there was fertile soil for crops and open spaces for herds, the cost of land remained well below what it would have been had the increasing demand for raw materials not have been met by simply opening more and more land.

William Cronon's remarkable study of the growth of the internal market that surrounded Chicago is a blueprint of how industrialization led to increasing exchange and commercial relations between a major manufacturing center and its frontier hinterland. And what emerges from his narrative is the degree to which wilderness and settlement weren't antagonistic to one another, but actually existed in a mutually-dependent state. But what the book does not reveal is the extent to which what happened to the most extreme extent in Chicago also happened at every point in the United States where frontier or wilderness was transformed into settled space. For example, in 1840 only one city of the largest 100 U.S. cities was located west of the Mississippi, in other words, the territory added after the Louisiana Purchase in 1802. By 1890 the number of the hundred largest cities west of the Mississippi had increased to 19, located in 11 different states. All of these cities, places like Denver, Omaha, Salt Lake City and Sioux City were connected to larger markets by rail, and all of them were points of trans-shipment for raw materials moving to manufacture or finished products destined for farms and homes.

Meanwhile, further to the east, beginning in the 1850's, manufacturing began emerging in smaller towns that a generation earlier had stood at the edge of civilization, but whose economic and demographic growth now created a demand for labor that went beyond working on farms. The town of Monroe, Massachusetts, for example, was originally settled by farmers who moved out from the coast around Boston around the turn of the century, lured by cheap, relatively flat farmland on what was called the Monroe Plateau. In the 1840's a second wave of settlers came to Monroe, most of whom found work building the Hoosac Railroad Tunnel which eventually connected rail-lines from Boston with commercial centers in upstate New York. The tunnel was completed in 1876, by which time a paper mill was already functioning and offering employment in the town of Monroe.

Paper mill (now abandoned) in Monroe, MA

In a period of roughly eighty years, Monroe moved from being on the edge of the wilderness to becoming a farming community and then an industrial center which, with the exception of the abandoned factory building on the bank of the Deerfield River, bears little relation to the way the town looks today. There are dead or half-dead towns like Monroe all over New England for which local and state governments have largely been unable to find either resources or strategies to bring them back to life. On rare occasions, the combination of scenic beauty or unique history turns a few such places into tourist and travel destinations, but most of them just continue to molder and fade away. Ironically, they often attract outdoor sportsmen who spend a few days and a few dollars taking advantage of the lack of population, because the absence of permanent residents provokes a return of wild fish and game.

The desertion and disappearance of the original factory towns, what is called re-ruralization, brings to full cycle the growth and development of America as it passed from wilderness to occupied zones and now in many of the latter places appears to be returning to its former, unoccupied state. That today's hunters would be the people who value the existence of such places is an ironic comment, given the extent to which their understanding and exploitation of unsettled and wilderness spaces is what gave birth to the existence of these small towns in the first place. Can the cycle start over again? Let's see in the next chapter what Rachel Carson had to say about that.

Chapter 4

Silent Spring

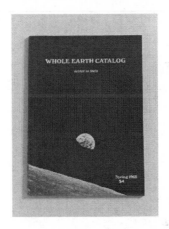

Readers who are old enough to remember the Whole Earth Catalog are probably wondering why it's in a book about guns. But in order to understand how the conservation movement founded by hunters like Teddy Roosevelt morphed into the environmental movement and left the hunters behind, we have to go back to the early 1960's, when the great coalition created by Roosevelt to conserve natural habitat began to fall apart.

Let's remember from Chapter Two that while the aim of early conservationists was to preserve areas in their natural state, the definition of which areas would be protected in this manner was fairly narrow. True, by a stroke of his presidential pen, Roosevelt was able to create millions of acres of protected woodland, as well as several nature preserves. And given the degree to which protection of any natural landscape prior to Roosevelt had been accomplished, his efforts in this respect should not be underestimated or ignored. But when one considers that Roosevelt's efforts resulted in less than 3 million acres being protected out of more than 2.3 *billion* acres, which does not include Hawaii or Alaska, the picture begins to change. And don't forget that almost all of this acreage was designated as national forest land which, although protected, really meant regulated, so that loggers and other commercial ventures would continue to have access to the resources in these forests both above and below ground.

This situation didn't change to any great degree with the creation of the National Park System in 1919. Once again, the total amount of land that was wholly protected from exploitation was a small fraction of the land mass from sea to shining sea, and with the exception of the parks themselves, most of what was otherwise considered federal park, recreation or preserve lands was managed, rather than protected from exploitation by commercial interests, including farmers, herders, mining companies and the like. And while the federal government today lays claim to roughly 650 million acres, almost all of this territory is concentrated in the ten most western states (plus Alaska), and most of this expanse is occupied by military installations or testing centers such as the infamous Area 51. In smaller, older states, particularly in the East, federal ownership of land falls under one percent.

From the beginning of the conservation movement, the effort to preserve natural species was more a function of regulating hunting and outdoor sports, rather than setting aside vast tracts of land and water for animal and fish habitats. Thus, organizations like Boone & Crockett primarily engaged in campaigns to promote standardized hunting seasons within different states so that animal and bird populations wouldn't become depleted, just because migration patterns crossed state boundaries and allowed hunters to take advantage of different laws or lack of laws in pursuing their sport. On the other hand, the conservation movement did not usually challenge the right of property owners to exploit property for commercial purposes, even if such activities cut down the amount of open space inhabited by wild species.

But what if protecting habitat was no longer directed at preserving animal life and instead was directed at preserving human life? This was the great change that began to take place in the 1960's, and it broke apart the broad coalition created at the end of the nineteenth century by Roosevelt and other conservationists with the appearance of environmentalism. Although the government had begun to react legislatively to environmental threats after World War II, it was the appearance in 1962 of Rachel Carson's extraordinary work, *Silent Spring*, that changed the entire trajectory of the discussion. Now the problem was defined not in terms of regulating natural habitat for the preservation of animal species, but rather regulating the human habitat which embraced everything; i.e., the whole Earth.

Carson was a zoologist and journalist whose earlier book, *The Sea Around Us*, demonstrated her ability to capture and excite the popular imagination in works about the natural environment. But *Silent Spring* wasn't so much a study of the environment as an agenda-laden attack on industrial pollutants in general and the chemical industry in particular. I speak of Carson's 'agenda' not so much to characterize her approach from a political perspective, but rather to underscore the degree to which she used scientific evidence not just to explain natural phenomena, but to advance an argument with specific goals in mind. In her case, the goals were to rid the environment of toxic chemicals that, in many cases, were introduced as the by-product of emerging industrial technologies, or were being used to enhance plant and farm productivity.

More than anything, what probably propelled Carson's work to the forefront of national consciousness was the immediate and energetic campaign by the chemical industry to denigrate her research and dismiss her claims. Even before *Silent Spring* was published, chemical companies like DuPont began mounting a PR and lobbying campaign against the book, correctly believing that Carson's contacts within the federal government (she had been an employee of the U.S. Department of Fisheries and later conducted research at the NIH) would spark an effort to ban or greatly reduce the use of DDT and other pesticides. Between the publicity generated by industry efforts to defend pesticide use, plus an enormously-popular serialized version of the book in *The New Yorker* Magazine, the basic approach and conclusions of Carson's work provoked a national concern about threats to the environment.

Although Carson would not live to see how the publication of *Silent Spring* would become the springboard of a national environmental movement, there is no doubt that the public and political response to her writings marked a major shift in thinking about how and why to preserve natural space. This was due in part to Carson's ability to explain complicated, scientific phenomena in simple, easy-to-grasp terms without losing the essence of the argument. What made the book so compelling was her ability to make readers understand the organic wholeness of the environment, and the degree to which introducing anything harmful into any part would create risks for everyone who came into contact with it. And if the environment was defined as the Earth, the whole Earth, then nobody on the Earth would be safe from pollutants and poisons introduced to any part of the planet.

A second factor that contributed to the strength of Carson's argument was its timeliness. To begin, the book was published at the same time that America was once again seeking to explore and tame a frontier; i.e., the New Frontier as enunciated by the Kennedy Administration, in particular the race against the Soviet Union to conquer space. It wasn't by accident that the first issue of the *Whole Earth Catalog*, published in 1968, would have the remarkable picture of the Earth taken from the moon. Much of the ethos of the Kennedy's New Frontier revolved around the idea of "making things better," for example, the concepts that stood behind the Peace Corps, but Kennedy was also concerned about environmental threats and quickly attached himself to Carson's crusade for cleaner and healthier land, air and water. As Douglas Brinkley noted in an article about Rachel Carson in *Audubon Magazine*, as a result of the coincidence of her efforts alongside Kennedy's New Frontier progressivism, conservation was no longer about protecting natural environments, it was about protecting everyone's health from things that threatened everyone's environment.

The new environmental movement, which took root with Carson's book, then began to flourish in the late 1960s as the first post-War generation began to graduate from college and a large and educated middle-class population appeared. For the first time in the history of the country the population included a large and growing segment of educated citizens who had the financial wherewithal and stability to think about quality of life rather than just the material quantities. And this was also the first time that, thanks to the mass communication technology of television, the entire society could begin to engage in discussions about national issues that might be far away from them in a physical or geographic sense, but were in fact not further away from the space between the couch on which they sat and the television set against the opposite wall. Thinking about environmental issues was no longer an abstract proposition, because the whole natural environment was now available to be viewed.

Alongside the intellectual and programmatic content of environmentalism was also a new strategy based on public advocacy which soon became a staple of all organizations that sought change through debate in the public arena. The *Whole Earth* magazine helped ignite national movements to clean up the air, the ground, the water, food, and everything else which might be contaminated due to excessive and unchecked economic growth. If the content of the environmental movement was first defined by the *Whole Earth* magazine in 1968, then the movement's strategy came to fruition with the first national Earth Day rallies in 1970. This event was largely the brainchild of a liberal U.S. Senator from Wisconsin (where the Progressive movement started) named Gaylord Nelson, who helped organize public events in cities and towns across the country, and used the momentum of this activity to forge a bi-partisan coalition on Capitol Hill that resulted in the creation of the Environmental Protection Agency in 1970.

Was the environmental movement anti-capitalist, as some of its critics charged and still charge? To the degree that the movement wanted to place more stringent controls on the environmental behavior of corporations, one could argue that any business regulation by definition is intrinsically anti-capitalist. But the impetus, style and strategies of environmental advocacy didn't grow out of any previous experience that challenged the economic underpinnings of the system, rather it grew out of the protests and group rallies that promoted civil rights and called for ending the Vietnam War.

The decade that spanned the mid-60's through the mid-70's saw a resurgence of liberal and progressive advocacy and protests that had not been experienced since the country came together and fought the Second World War. I was a student, first in college in New York City, then in graduate school in Chicago, from 1962 until 1971. I do not recall a single week during that entire ten-year period that some group wasn't protesting or marching, be it for civil rights, women's equality, anti-war, ending nuclear testing, environmentalism, or all of the aforementioned rolled into one. What follows is a brief anecdote that sums up the tenor of the times.

I drove across the country in September, 1968 and at one point got a flat tire as I was going through the Rosebud Indian Reservation outside of Rapid City, South Dakota. At the time the reservation was the scene of a modern version of Cowboys and Indians, with the cowboys being played by the FBI and the Indians being played by members of the American Indian Movement (AIM) led by Russell Means. Just as I had finished changing the tire a car pulled up with three heavily-armed FBI agents inside. One of them stuck his head out the window and asked if I needed any help. When I told them that I was about the get back in the car and drive into town to get the flat fixed, one of them said, "Just remember, if you see any pickup trucks on this road, don't slow down because when they see you're white they might try to shoot." And off they went.

The FBI guys left me sitting in the middle of beautiful prairie, in fact about ten miles from a point in Custer State Park that is considered the only piece of totally virgin prairie still left in the United States. The sun was beginning to go down behind the buttes, the colors were remarkable, so I sat there next to my car for a bit just taking it all in. All of a sudden a pickup truck swung by, slowed and jackknifed a little further up the road and slowly came back towards my car. There were two Indians in the truck and as their vehicle pulled up in front of mine, I waved and they waved back. We ended up standing along the road having a nice chat and they even told me which gasoline station in town would give me the best service for repairing my flat.

Why was the meeting with these two Indians, who were members of AIM out patrolling the reservation, so different from what the FBI guys had led me to expect? Because I had student-length hair, my car had Illinois license plates because I was in graduate school in Chicago, and the two young Indian men wanted to hear all about the "riots" that had taken place during the Democratic Convention that had come to an end the week before I left to go on my cross-country trip. The fact that I had participated in the demonstrations, had actually smelled tear gas and seen some of the Chicago cops go swarming through Lincoln Park gave me an instant credibility with these two kids with whom I was sitting and talking on the Great Plains.

In some vague way or another, my presence outside the Democratic Convention and their membership in AIM put us on the same side. And if you were a college student on just about any campus anywhere in the United States between the mid-sixties and the early seventies, if you weren't involved in some kind of liberal or progressive political activity, or at least were a witness to the same, you weren't on a college campus. Even the most stalwart, conservative schools like Notre Dame and Brigham Young had demonstrations against the war. And when the war came to its inglorious end, the same sentiment manifested itself in concerns and demonstrations and movements for environmental causes and the like.

Much of this campus political activity had to do with a dramatic growth in college enrollments during the same period. In 1950, less than 30% of eighteen and nineteen-year olds were enrolled in college, a percentage of this age group that grew to slightly more than 50% by 1968. This increase in the number of students attending college was true for every age group and reflected the extent to which more and more American families could afford to send children to college rather than sending them into the workforce because they needed the additional wage. And while minority populations lagged behind whites in terms of college enrollments, even the percentage of Black youngsters ages 18-19 who were in college increased from 20% to nearly 40% during the same period.

The college-age population that emerged in the 1960's (and the faculty who taught them) was imbued with the liberalism of JFK and his New Frontier. They were also, for the first time, a significant economic and demographic force whose presence could be measured both in terms of the ballot box and the consumer market. And their preferences for consumer items and lifestyle consumption were decidedly encompassed by the philosophy and direction of the environmental movement. Even though he is usually not mentioned in recountings of the emergence of environmentalism, probably the single most influential figure at the time was Ralph Nader, whose 1965 book, *Unsafe at Any Speed,* created an awareness of the dangers that might arise from the pursuit of profits unchecked by concerns about consumer safety. And while Nader's book focused on the attempt by General Motors to cover up the engineering faults of a small, rear-engine car known as the Chevrolet Corvair, the most popular automobile found on college campuses was another compact, rear-engine vehicle known as the Volkswagen Beetle.

Where are the Beach Boys?

The Beetle became the defining cultural icon of a generation of college students at the same time that Detroit was turning its back on cars that were safer and fuel-efficient, while, beginning in the 1970s, the price of gasoline started to become a newsworthy issue as well. Somehow, smaller and more efficient caught the mood of the times, and it was a mood most particularly felt among younger, college-educated kids who were defining themselves differently from the older, World War II generation which had fought the great fight thirty years earlier but then led us into the catastrophe known as Vietnam. And let's not forget the fact that it was also college campuses in the 60's that provided the recruiting environments not for the military, as scores and scores of ROTC programs were forced to do business in off-campus locations, but recruiting grounds for freedom rides and other forms of non-violent actions that continued all the way through and past the passage of the Civil Rights Act in 1968.

Thus, a combination of anti-war, civil rights, feminism and other liberal causes all combined to create a ferment of advocacy that was also a substantial contributor to the ecology movement. At the same time there was also something else at work which shaped the political and social outlook of the period, and that had to do with the ending of the military draft. The first law covering military conscription was passed in 1917 due to manpower requirements of World War I. The draft was discontinued in 1920 but was reborn with a new law passed in 1940 that required all males between 18 and 65 to register and allowed the government to actually place into active service all males between 18 and 65 for a period of 18 months, which was then extended to 24 months and, in 1942, extended for the duration of the war.

This law was replaced by a new law in 1948 that required universal male registration and gave the government the right to press into service all males between the ages of 19 and 26. The law continued previous selective service laws that granted exemptions for such things as hardships, number of family dependents, as well as deferments for certain types of status, including full-time college enrollment. This law, with various amendments and revisions, remained in effect until 1973, when then-Defense Secretary Melvin Laird announced its termination and replacement by an all-volunteer army, which remains in effect to the present day. But from a social perspective, the end of the draft which had been in existence for more than 40 years not only meant that almost all men and women would never experience armed training, it also meant the end of the great social equalizer that selective service represented from the time the draft was first introduced.

The end of selective service meant the end of a military training experience that had been nearly universal for every male who came of age between 1940 and 1973. And the lack of military training meant that as the next generation came of age, they might do so without the experience of having fired a gun. If they lived in rural areas, as we shall see in the following chapter, most had learned to shoot as they grew up and followed other family members or friends into the woods during a hunt. But if they were urban dwellers or suburban residents, which was the fastest-growing geographic demographic in the 1970's, they were not for the most part engaged in hunting, nor did they have any real occasion to handle firearms once they could escape the draft. And even when the draft was still in force prior to 1973, a combination of student deferments and other non-military options meant that if you went to college after high school the chances that you might wind up marching to and fro in boot camp were negligible to nil. I graduated from high school in 1962, all the white kids in my graduating class went on to college, and not a single one of them, with the exception of myself, ever opened their mailbox to receive the fateful letter that began with "Greetings from the President of the United States."

Meanwhile, at the same time that college campuses were spawning a generation that engaged in advocacy to promote various political, economic and social ideals, another advocacy campaign was also beginning to gather steam with the aim of stopping a particular political agenda from becoming law. What I'm referring to is the decision by the NRA to shift its primary energies away from hunting and training and begin building a membership whose task would be to advocate for fewer restrictions on the use of guns. This is not the place to engage in a long discussion about the history of the NRA; you can read the details of that story in my previous book, *Guns for Good Guys, Guns for Bad Guys.* Suffice it to say, however, that the events that led up to the Gun Control Act of 1968 marked the first time that the NRA began to move to center stage over the issue of ownership of guns.

Prior to that campaign, the organization took for granted the decision by some Americans to own guns which, in virtually all instances, grew out of the use of firearms for work on the farm, or for recreation and sport. In many respects in terms of the message and the audience, the pre-1960's NRA was little different from hunting organizations like Boone & Crockett, advising hunters about different types of guns and ammunition, promoting responsible marksmanship and regulated hunting, and tying the existence and ownership of guns to the selfsame legends and cultural stereotypes that glorified wilderness and the Old West.

Here's a membership ad that appeared for the NRA in 1957:

Note the appeal to sports minded hunters and shooters, outdoor hobbyists if you will, to have fun by joining an organization that, from this ad, has no political agenda at all. Nor did they need a political agenda, because in 1957 nobody was worried about guns. The tide didn't begin to turn until a few days after November 22, 1963 when it was revealed that Lee Harvey Oswald had purchased the gun with which he allegedly shot the President by sending a mail order check for thirteen bucks and change to a gun wholesaler in Chicago who then mailed him the gun.

Gun owners had been buying guns through the mail and from catalogs since we began moving across the country and the Sears, Roebuck catalog furnished virtually every item and implement that was kept in a home. And while the mail-order purchase of "concealable" weapons was banned by Congress in 1927, largely in response to urban violence that erupted in the wake of Prohibition, rifles and shotguns, as long as they were not fully-automatic weapons, were bought and sold like any other consumer item either over the counter in the local hardware store or through the mails. Here's an ad from the Sears catalog which calls the store "the world's largest gun store." Make no mistake about it, that statement was probably true. Note that the ad pictures the NRA "Official Target" as well.

Nobody, certainly not the NRA, was prepared for the firestorm about guns that was ignited by the events in Dallas in 1963. Kennedy was not the first President to be assassinated. In fact, he was the fourth President to die in office from a gunshot wound, the previous victim being William McKinley, whose death in 1901 brought Teddy Roosevelt onto center stage. But in the case of Kennedy, his death brought to a close a brief but heady experience for those college students of the 1960s who thought of themselves as members of a new, liberal crusade. And it was a crusade that, while it enlisted a new generation of college-educated kids, as well as many of their parents who came back from World War II and went to college on the GI Bill, was also a crusade that did not for the most part enlist a blue-collar constituency or the people, young and old, who were still on the farm.

Almost immediately after the assassination, Senator Thomas Dodd of Connecticut submitted a bill to the Senate to outlaw mail-order purchase of guns. The bill languished in committee and never made it to the floor of either chamber largely because of the fear that it might be a campaign issue in the 1964 election, probably the first instance in which the NRA was able to defeat a major piece of gun control legislation by summoning enough pro-gun sentiment in certain districts to keep a bill from becoming law. Anti-gun politics continued to bubble along as an issue of national concern, but it wasn't until the killings of Martin Luther King, Jr. and Robert Kennedy in 1968 that enough sentiment for gun control found its way into transforming debate into a law.

But even in the wake of these shootings and the national shock that was registered in many quarters, the vote to create the first national gun control system was extremely close, to the point that the initial tie vote that almost left the bill in both House and Senate committees was only undone with the personal intervention of Lyndon Johnson. Meanwhile, although the NRA came out in favor of the bill, continued agitation from within the ranks of the organization forced the leadership at the last moment to withdraw its support of the new law and make a public pledge to refrain from taking a position of future gun laws, no matter how benign.

At the same time that the NRA began to shift its energies towards responding to anti-gun legislation, the message to its membership also took on a clearly political tone. Here's an excerpt from the NRA's membership campaign that ran in 1970:

> As it has over the past 99 years, the big, strong, million-member National Rifle Association, acting in close concert with other leading non-profit organizations, is waging a continuing battle to preserve and protect, for now and for the future, the hunting rights, privileges and freedoms that many hunters take for granted.

> But it is highly dangerous to take what we *consider* an "inherent" right for granted these days! The opponents of individual freedoms press forward on every front. In the name of "gun control" they are waging an insidious war against the rights of *you* and every other responsible, law-abiding hunter and sports shooter.

By today's standards, the language in this NRA membership promotion is almost quaint, and the organization had yet to take on it current-day role as the protector and defender of the 2nd Amendment; note the vague reference to every individual's "rights," a word which today would never be mentioned without the 2nd Amendment qualifier attached. But there is a clear shift in emphasis from the 1957 membership promotion reproduced above, a shift that would become even more pronounced in the years that followed.

The move from protecting hunting to protecting gun ownership, as I'll explain in the chapter that follows, was partially in response to the fact that hunting sports were beginning to account for a smaller and smaller part of gun ownership while, at the same time, a generalized fear of crime and urban lawlessness was also gaining the upper hand. And what's important to remember here is that the 1970's, following the end of Vietnam, saw an eclipse of liberal idealism (after all, it was liberals in the Kennedy and Johnson Administrations who planned, prosecuted and ultimately lost Vietnam) and its replacement in popular political currency by the conservative movement that almost got Reagan nominated in 1976 and then propelled him to the presidency four years hence.

One year before Reagan came into office, however, the most significant environmental event in the United States took place not far from Harrisburg, PA, when the nuclear power plant at Three Mile Island suffered a partial meltdown of one of its reactors, resulting in the evacuation of more than 140,000 local residents. It was this event, more than any other, which propelled environmentalism to the forefront of the liberal advocacy agenda at the same time that support for this agenda began to erode as a more conservative mood throughout the country resulted in the Reagan 1980 triumph. The waning of environmental and other liberal causes during the late 1970's and into the early 1980's can be understood by comparing the record of Jimmy Carter's Interior Secretary, James Andrus, to the record of his successor James Watt. Andrus, who had been Governor of Idaho, brought an impressive environmental and conservationist record with him to the Carter Administration and while in Washington, among other achievements, was able to set aside more than 100 million natural acres in Alaska, which included the Arctic National Wildlife Refuge. Watt, on the other hand, who had previously served as a functionary of the U.S. Chamber of Commerce, made it clear that he saw his role primarily to manage leasing of federal lands to private mining, logging and other commercial interests. Among other remarkable quotes about the environment from Watt was the following: "My responsibility is to follow the Scriptures which call upon us to occupy the land until Jesus returns." That's right. A Cabinet officer actually made that statement in 1981.

Along with the slow but steady retreat of liberal advocacy during Reagan's ascendancy was the final collapse of the Democratic Party in the South and its replacement in virtually every state of the old Confederacy with a Republican Party that struck a decidedly more conservative tone, particularly in what came to be known as social "wedge" issues like abortion, public prayer and opposition to welfare and women's rights. The injection of a conservative social agenda into the political arena, justified as a reawakening of "traditional" American values, fit the growing politicization of the NRA and other gun-owning groups, in particular reflecting the fact that gun ownership was strongest amongst whites who lived in the South. How could the NRA fail to embrace conservative Republican ideas when a majority of the organization's membership lived in the region where those ideas took firmest root? During the two Reagan administrations, southern states that had not voted Republican since Reconstruction now found themselves sending Republicans to Washington to represent them in both chambers of Congress, and the NRA found it convenient to align itself with this emerging conservative tide that embraced social issues of greatest significance in the South.

Just beneath the surface of the social agenda that increasingly defined the political stance of the Republican Party under Reagan there lurked another, more visceral issue that would also spark the NRA's appeal to gun owners and this was the issue of race. It wasn't lost on anyone that Reagan's very first campaign speech after receiving the presidential nomination in 1980 took place not just in Mississippi, but in Philadelphia, Mississippi, the town in which three northern civil rights workers, Schwerner, Goodman and Chaney, had been brutally murdered by the Klan with the connivance of local law enforcement officials in 1964. Their murders and the aftermath, including several lengthy but inconclusive trials, became in many respects the iconic event that represented both the sacrifices and successes of the civil rights movement, as well as the resistance of whites to integration as it swept across the South. And here is a direct quote from that speech, with the words that many if not most southern whites were waiting for him to say: "I believe in state's rights; I believe in people doing as much as they can for themselves at the community level and at the private level."

What these words meant was that a generation of civil rights activism was coming to an end. And while Reagan could do very little, when all was said and done, to undo the 1965 voting rights act, the 1968 civil rights law and the other legal gains that had been achieved by blacks since the historic Brown decision in 1953, the tone and the tenor about race relations had decidedly changed. And nowhere was this change more evident than in issues related to race and crime. Because the truth is that Reagan's strength in the South was most noticeable among followers of George Wallace, and while Wallace did not make a presidential bid in 1980, he and his particular brand of racial politics and rhetoric were nevertheless a factor in the race. Reagan's constant references to the "welfare queen" driving around Chicago in her Cadillac or the "young buck" who used food stamps to buy T-bone steaks were enough to delight both Southern white audiences who were uncomfortable with integration and northern audiences comprised of white, industrial workers whose neighborhoods for the first time now contained blacks.

Working-class home ownership and the ability of blue collar families to move to the suburbs created a receptive audience in this demographic group for messages that played up fears about inner-city crime. And since the Republican Party had fared so well in this population by running a former actor who was a no-nonsense stand-up kind of a guy, the NRA figured they could learn from that experience too. So in the late 1980's the NRA began running its first membership ads that promoted the idea of carrying concealed weapons for protection against crime, and the ads were clearly aimed at evoking fears about crime that were associated with inner-city streets. They also hired Charlton Heston, who would later become NRA President and made his famous "from my cold, dead hands" speech at the 1990 NRA Convention, to appear in television ads that showed him walking down a dark and scary street in what was alleged to be DC, telling the viewers that the streets were "ruled by criminals" and that "our leaders" wanted to ban guns but not do anything to put criminals behind bars.

These ads and others were an overt attempt to define law-abiding gun ownership not as a constitutional issue, but as a way to distinguish between "right" and "wrong" in every aspect of political life. By changing their orientation away from protecting gun ownership for hunters to promoting gun ownership as a response to inner-city crime, the NRA was taking a calculated gamble that the rhetoric of the Reagan majority would remain a fixture in the mainstream dialog of American political life. The NRA's shift was also a reflection of the degree to which, as I will explain in Chapter 5, the recognition that hunting and hunters were on the wane. It didn't take rocket science for the NRA to figure out that appeals to gun ownership (and NRA membership) on the basis of outdoor sporting activities would ultimately become a dead end.

Meanwhile, just as NRA membership and gun ownership in general was becoming increasingly stratified towards whites living in rural communities and smaller cities and towns, so the newly-emerging, largely suburban and urban middle class was becoming distanced from the social milieu in which gun owners tended to be found. Not only was America becoming more middle class, it was also becoming more educated, and with education came concerns about quality of life that had no room for an interest in guns. And when President Clinton pushed through a crime bill in 1994 that reflected the country's growing unease about lawlessness in urban environments, the bill was tied to a major expansion of federal gun control laws which included both a ten-year ban on high-capacity magazines and an instant background check for all gun purchases conducted through over-the-counter sales.

The NRA fought and lost both of those legislative battles, and in the aftermath realized that its strategy of detaching itself from hunters and barricading gun rights behind the shield of personal defense, had, in fact, not gone far enough. And what became the vehicle for the further growth of pro-gun sentiment, at a time when the actual numbers of gun owners was going down, was an all-out assault on anything and anyone who might be construed as undermining 2nd Amendment rights. This was a brilliant marketing stroke, when all is said and done, because at a time when America was becoming the world's most prolific consumer economy, guns were the only consumer item afforded explicit protection by the Bill of Rights. Now, whether the Constitution protected the actual ownership of guns, as opposed to the "right" to self-defense, wouldn't be settled by the Supreme Court until 2008. But the fact that guns were important enough to be mentioned in virtually the next sentence after the enumeration of such sacred rights as free speech, free assembly and a free press, gave the defenders of the 2nd Amendment a basis for mobilizing gun ownership sentiment that was a marketer's dream. Not only were defenders of the 2nd Amendment true patriots, given that they were fighting to uphold our country's most sacred historical and legal text, they were also now in the forefront of the defense of civil rights since, after all, what could be a more important civil right than one enumerated in the Bill of Rights? Thus, even before Charlton Heston agreed to serve as NRA President beginning in 2000, he announced a three-year "crusade" to teach America's children the value of the 2nd Amendment, or what he referred to as our "first freedom."

Because gun
rights are lost
on our kids.

But notwithstanding the cleverness and
timeliness of this marketing scheme, the problem
was that Heston and the NRA spent a lot of
money preaching to an audience that was not
necessarily NRA members, but were already gun
owners. And while there's no doubt that the size
of the NRA membership has grown substantially
over the past twenty years (my estimate is that the
total number has doubled from two to four
million), the percentage of American households
in which guns can be found keeps going down.
Which means that gun owners, notwithstanding
how vocal they can be, continue to represent a
smaller and smaller percentage of the population,
and within that population, as I will show in the
chapter that follows, hunters represent an
increasingly smaller percentage as well.

Meanwhile, the environmental movement and the whole notion of environmentalism continue to grow. Not only do we accept the notion that the environment embraces the entire planet as well as the atmosphere, but a majority of Americans also believe that government should play an active role in managing environmental affairs. This becomes a difficult problem for the hunting community, because in most instances they are represented by an organization that prides itself on its efforts to limit the role of government in anything that has to do with guns, as well as just about anything else. And while recent events demonstrate that the NRA is able to put the brakes on governmental efforts to expand gun control at the federal level, when it comes to the concerns of hunters, the first real contest between hunter-conservationists on the one hand and environmentalists on the other ended up as a clear victory for the latter group.

The contest took place in California, ironically and coincidentally the location of the first environmental battle in 1908 known as the Hetch-Hetchy Dam Project, between the State of California and the Sierra Club led by John Muir. The law, approved by Jerry Brown in October, 2013, effectively banned lead shot from being used for hunting, spreading a lead ammunition ban that had already been in existence in areas that were habitat for the California Condor. But an even greater irony than the fact that this environmental battle took place where modern environmentalism was born was the fact that hunting organizations and publications were this time unanimous in their opposition to the law, whereas it was an article in Forest and Stream Magazine, authored by George Bird Grinnell in 1894, that first mentioned "the destruction of ducks, geese and swans" by the toxic effects of lead ammunition.

Grinnell, along with Roosevelt, later founded the Audubon Society, which was one of the chief supporters of the California lead-banning law. And while opponents of the measure, including the NRA, claimed that the law was aimed not just at banning lead ammunition but banning hunting (as a first step to banning firearms), the passage was not really in doubt, largely because the toxicity of lead had long been established by other public health campaigns, in particular banning lead from paint that could be ingested by kids. It was also the case that lead ammunition bans had been enacted in various localities throughout the United States, particularly along eastern coastal flyways, and ammunition manufacturers had responded over the years by bringing a wide variety of steel-component ammunition to the market that could be used in lieu of lead.

Behind the debate, however, was another factor that demonstrates the division between hunter-conservationists on the one hand, and environmentalists on the other. The main argument made by opponents of the law was that forcing hunters to forego the use of lead ammunition would make the sport more expensive, because steel-based ammunition was substantially more costly. And to the degree that hunting was and is a blue-collar sport, there was some truth to this point of view. Ammunition is already subject to an 11% federal excise tax that is paid by the manufacturers and then passed on to consumers, funds which go directly into conservation and habitat programs run by the states and the feds. Requiring hunters to pay a premium for ammunition by eliminating the cheaper lead loads is, in effect, discriminating against them from a financial point of view.

On the other hand, the environmental movement long ago arrived at a consensus as regards its willingness to pay the extra costs of cleaner soil, cleaner food and cleaner air. And to the degree that environmentalists, as opposed to hunters, did not find it difficult to justify using personal resources to protect us all from toxic waste, this was a perfect reflection of the social and class divisions that began moving hunters and environmentalists in different directions once the environmental movement began to define habitat as a place that was occupied by more than just birds, fish and animals. As I will explain in the next chapter, the social and economic divisions that began to emerge between different populations within the United States were not so much reflected in terms of gun ownership versus non-gun ownership; they were much more a function of the growing gap between hunters and environmentalists, the former who saw nature as a place where they could safely shoot living things, the latter who saw nature as a place to explore with a kayak, not with a gun.

It was Teddy Roosevelt, the man who first encouraged hunters to become conservationists, who saw portents of the conflict between managing as opposed to preserving natural ecosystems. In 1902 he was the first (and last) President to publish a book while in office, in this case The Deer Family, which he co-authored with three other pre-eminent naturalists, T.S. Van

Dyke, Daniel Elliott and A. J. Stone. The four chapters written by Roosevelt were part reminiscence, part exhortation and part instruction. They were also, as Douglas Brinkley has stated, possibly "the most important of all Roosevelt's books for our understanding of his evolved views on conservation."

In this book Roosevelt explicitly voiced his concerns about the need to balance conservation of habitat to sustain animal herds with preservation of the natural environment to afford everyone their particular type of outdoor enjoyment. For Roosevelt, it came down to a question of access, described as follows:

> "Most of us, as we grow older, grow to care relatively less for the sport itself than for the splendid freedom and abounding health of outdoor life in the woods, on the plains, and among the great mountains; and to the true nature lover it is melancholy to see the wilderness stripped of the wild creatures which gave it no small part of its peculiar charm."

And to the extent that hunters would have access to areas that might still be too difficult to afford the average person the same degree of movement and penetration required for the taking of game,

> "the big game hunter should be a field naturalist. If possible, he should be an adept with the camera ; and hunting with the camera will tax his skill far more than hunting with the rifle, while the results in the long run give much greater satisfaction. Wherever possible he should keep a note-book, and should carefully study and record the habits of the wild creatures, especially when in some remote regions to which trained scientific observers but rarely have access."

More than a century before hunting organizations like Ducks Unlimited and environmental groups like Audubon squared off for the battle over using lead ammunition, Roosevelt realized that the way to avoid a conflict between management of hunting habitat and preservation of wilderness was to invest hunters with responsibilities for both. Of course for someone of his background, such an approach made common sense. After all, it was the task of the nation's elite to set and maintain the proper forms of behavior for the common man who would then follow in their wake. How could Roosevelt ever imagine that today's hunters would see the 'elite' not as their benign exemplars but as their greatest foe? For that matter, could he ever have considered the possibility that hunting would no longer be a mark of distinction and definition for the upper class? The chapter which follows attempts to answer both questions – and more.

CHAPTER 5

WHERE ARE THE HUNTERS?

Normal Rockwell

I'll start this chapter with a brief remembrance from my childhood. I was born and raised in Washington, D.C., my parents having moved from New York City to DC because my father went to work for the Federal Government just before the outbreak of the Second World War. By the time I was a young adolescent in the mid-50's, he had left government service and moved into private industry. We lived in the District, as we called it, and my parents' circle of friends, like my mother and father, were educated professionals who were also in the private sector or had remained as government employees, for the most part attorneys working for the various Federal agencies.

The Federal Government in those days was much different than what it is now, as was the country, for that matter. It consisted of a handful of Cabinet agencies (the great expansion of the Cabinet took place under a Republican named Nixon) of which the largest was the Department of Defense, which, if it hadn't been for the mess in Korea, wouldn't have known what to do with the white elephant building known as the Pentagon. All of the Cabinet agencies were located in an area known as the Federal Triangle, midway between the Capitol and the White House on Pennsylvania Avenue, a group of hideously ugly sandstone buildings built during WPA and housing, among other things, a wonderful aquarium in the basement of the Interior Department. The Smithsonian, the country's museum, was housed in an old, red-block fortress-like building on the south side of the mall which contained, among other things, Franklin Roosevelt's stamp collection, while buildings like the NASA museum, the Hirshhorn, the National Gallery, the American History Museum were all way off in the future. The Vice

President lived in an apartment on Connecticut Avenue, walking distance to the National Zoo, and once I was in the zoo with my mother who pointed out Pat, Tricia and Julie Nixon standing by themselves on the other side of the sea lion pool.

I am convinced that the real growth of government was primarily the result of air-conditioning. Because before all these government buildings had air-conditioning systems, Washington was a place that you did your best to escape from by the beginning of June. So Congress did its best to get its work done before the Summer, and since every other year was an election, most of the Senators and Representatives didn't want to come back to town after Labor Day anyway. This may sound like a very quaint way to analyze how and why government has changed over the last fifty years, but I can tell you that if the seat of the Federal Government had remained in New York, where it was once located, albeit briefly, chances are that it would have been much larger much earlier because New York usually has a short and tolerable Summer season.

Not so DC. Beginning in May we usually slept on sheets laid out on the floor, somehow sweltered through the last days of school in June, and then packed up the house and took off for either the Chesapeake shore or the mountains to the west or north. In 1954 my father rented a summer escape for us in the little town of Sabilasville, Maryland, which was in the Catoctin Mountains on the Maryland-Pennsylvania border, right down the road from the entrance to Camp David, about 60 miles from DC. In terms of the local population, however, we could have been 60,000 miles away from the Nation's Capitol, as it was called.

The first thing my mother did was unpack the car. The second thing she did was hire one of the local gals to come in every day and clean up. After all, everyone in my parents' circle had a full-time maid, and the fact that we were encamped out in the country for the summer didn't mean that my mother should do without her usual amenities. She didn't have to go far to find a household servant, however, because by the time the car was unpacked, our arrival had already attracted a group of local denizens who stood alongside the driveway leading up to the house, staring at us the way that the Indians probably gawked when first setting their eyes on Captain Cook.

In short order my mother hired a domestic staff, consisting of Billie, whom I found quite interesting because she didn't appear to have any teeth, and her husband whose name I don't recall, whose tasks included cutting the lawn, puttering around here and there, and telling me about the time he and *his* father drove to Philadelphia to see Dizzy Dean. I also recall that the property had a cement block about two feet square, with the seal of Lord Baltimore on one side and the coat of arms of William Penn on the other, with a few chunks missing because various souvenir-hunters had evidently wanted to add a piece of an original Mason-Dixon marker to their personal collections of Americana.

No sooner were Billie and her husband engaged as loyal family retainers, then I was invited to walk over to their shack to meet and begin playing with their kids. I don't remember exactly the size of the brood, although I was impressed by the number of brats that were running around the premises, such as they were. But what really got me excited was when I walked into the living room and saw five or six shotguns and rifles stacked against the wall. I was no stranger to guns, in fact my prized possession at home was a Daisy Red Ryder BB gun with which I tried to hit the squirrels that lived in a tree in our backyard. But these weren't BB guns, these were real guns, and they were used to kill not only squirrels, but white-tail deer, of which there were also some antler pairs hung up on the walls.

The most interesting thing about those guns was not that they were in the house per se, nor that they were sitting there in open view. It was the fact that I was the only one who seemed to notice them. Which, when all is said and done, is what truly distinguished my social background from the people who lived in that house. And over the course of the summer I probably was inside a dozen or more homes around the village of Sabilasville, and every one of these residences had the same stack of guns sitting against a wall, or hung on pegs, or otherwise lying around one way or another in plain view. The interior of my home in DC might have been furnished with greater attention to style and detail, the walls were covered with beautiful wallpaper rather than rolled-on paint, we had full bookcases instead of a wooden crate standing on its end, wall-to-wall carpeting rather than linoleum and so forth. But these were differences of taste backed up by urban sophistication and cash. The one and the only real difference in the interior of our fancy home in the city and their shacks in the country was that *they had guns and we didn't.*

I make this point at the beginning of the chapter on hunting because if you took the trouble to buy and read this book, the chances are likely that you were raised in a home much like mine, rather than in a home lived in by Billie, her husband and their brood. Because, like it or not, hunting as a hobby or even as a commercial venture was almost always, notwithstanding Teddy Roosevelt and the other founders of the Boone and Crockett Club, a pursuit engaged in by the common folk. In fact, if the settlement of America meant the expansion of what had been British traditions to the New World, the one British practice that did not get transplanted to any great degree in America was the extent to which hunting was denied to anyone except the titled and the wealthy, whose titles and wealth were a function of the ownership of land.

In England much of the forest land was considered part of the royal patrimony, and even though many of the medieval prohibitions on farming or hunting in these territories had fallen by the wayside, the custom of limiting hunting access to a chosen few not only was part of British culture, but even survived in many woodland regions throughout the realm. The map below represents what many believe to have been the location of such restricted territories as late as the fourteenth century, and it clearly demonstrates the degree to which there was a continuation of limiting hunting access in virtually every part of the British Isles.

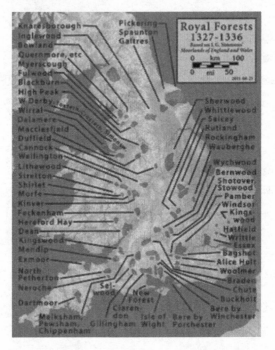

And this map only shows royal preserves; the degree to which the titled nobility possessed landed domains was far greater than what the Crown itself possessed, but like royal lands the land owned by the aristocracy was also protected from hunting by commoners. Thus, while royal and aristocratic land was often rented out for farming purposes to local residents, it was not customary to extend the same rental concessions to hunting, which was considered a sport for the upper and privileged classes. From the Middle Ages onward, it was traditional to let residents on the manor work much of the farmland in common, give a portion of the harvest over to the manor lord and keep the remainder either for themselves or to send to the market. And even when manorial estates started to be broken up and sold off as private property, the tradition of common farming remained very much alive in England and the Continent.

But common access to farmland was one thing, common access to hunting land quite another. It was actually this distinction between using land for farming as opposed to hunting that led to the use of the word 'poaching' which first appeared in the Middle Ages and meant 'bagging' in the sense of enclosing something in a bag so that its identity could be hidden from view. Poaching, which was actually a form of landed smuggling, was considered a serious crime in England and in some circumstances was punishable by disfigurement or even death. The fact that poachers were carrying off animals that served not so much as a primary source of food but as a trophy for a royal or aristocratic hunt only underscored the degree to which hunting and access to wildlife was so clearly a function of social status and social class.

British law abounds with examples of the extent to which hunting was reserved for the high and mighty, and proscribed for anyone and everyone who was not a member of the landed gentry or above. An act in 1670 forbade the killing even of rabbits unless it was done by a manor lord or someone with substantial income from property. Individuals who purchased estates, rather than receiving them through inheritance, could hunt on their own lands if they could show an annual income in excess of 100 pounds, which might seem like nothing today but in pre-industrial era represented ten times the annual income of a farm worker.

Along with laws that disqualified just about everyone from hunting were also laws that allowed members of the privileged class to exercise "free chase" and "free warren," which basically meant that a lord could chase game animals through fields planted by the local folk but could not be held liable if the hunting activity destroyed or damaged local crops. When young Theodore Roosevelt went galloping across Wyoming in search of buffalo and bear, he didn't have to worry about trampling the plantings because farmers hadn't yet begun to cultivate anything but a few isolated fields. Luckily, had he lived in England in the previous century, it wouldn't have mattered whether or not his trusty steed tore up the tilled soil and crops underneath.

Roosevelt was also quite enamored of the fact that hunting, particularly in the Great Plains fashion, built character, strength and a keen sense of self-worth. He frequently said that he would never have been able to be the Chief Executive had he not learned self-reliance and clarity of purpose by going hunting out on the range. In that respect, he also shared some basic assumptions with his aristocratic British forebears about the value of hunting as a way to develop good behavior, a workmanlike ethos and a constraint on otherwise useless endeavors. As quoted in a brilliant article by Douglas Hay (from the book Albion's Fatal Tree), laws prohibiting hunting by commoners protected the poor from their own "idleness" and therefore was the essence of good government. If the farm laborer could wander off into the woods, who would remain behind to till the fields, gather the harvest and work the land?

But the most egregious example of how class and social standing was reflected in laws covering hunting was the infamous "Black Act" passed by Parliament in 1723. The law, which was provoked by a series of attacks by poaching gangs operating in various forest areas, prohibited going into any forest wearing a disguise that would hinder identification, and it also created harsh penalties, including capitol punishments, for persons convicted of poaching or other unauthorized activity in forests. The word 'black' referred to the fact that the poachers blackened their faces with charcoal so that they wouldn't be identified if seen by witnesses in the woodlands.

The Black Act and several other draconian laws were eventually overturned at the beginning of the nineteenth century, but nobody who journeyed from England to settle in the American colonies (included those poor wretches who were sentenced to transportation because they violated gaming laws) was unaware of the extent to which hunting and, for that matter, the use of land in general was tightly bound up in laws, regulations and customs that reflected a social order based on heredity and class. But once coastal regions were settled by the early colonists, a vast, open and largely free woodland in which they could hunt was right at hand. And this remained the case all the way through the colonial period and into the founding of the country, with open range available for hunting up to the end of the nineteenth century. For most Americans the open woods and ranges represented a hunting environment that was totally different from the traditions and practices that still remained in force throughout England and the European Continent. What Roosevelt referred to (in The Deer Family) as the "admirably sportsmanlike English spirit" in hunting was not a democratic spirit in the way he wished it to be.

In this respect, more than any other, American hunting and American hunters reflected the absence of social class distinctions and traditions that were so common in England and other Old World zones. Because again, it must be remembered that the hunters and farmers who settled the American frontier did so at the same time that the industrial revolution created a market for the animals they slaughtered and the crops they harvested to the point that farming and hunting became one and the same kind of activity. If you lived outside the big cities you farmed but you also hunted and suffered few of the difficulties of access or boundary rights that were typical of environments where open land was scarce. It's difficult to imagine today that as recently as fifty years ago, within the lifetime of many people still alive (like myself) that one could wander off into the woods and hunt unmolested, yet be standing less than a two-hour drive from urban centers that contained millions of people. This was the hunting legacy that most Americans living in rural zones enjoyed through the first half of the twentieth century. And as that century wore on, it wasn't the lack of land or the difficulties of access that made hunting a less-frequent form of sport. It was the lack of hunters themselves.

When the U.S. Census declared, in 1890, that the frontier was closed, a majority of Americans still lived in small towns or on farms. In fact, of the more than 62 million Americans enumerated (and perhaps slightly undercounted) in that census, more than two-thirds, more than 40 million, still lived in what we would call rural zones. Today the census classifies the "rural" population as roughly 20% of the country's total numbers, but as late as 1970 the rural population; i.e., those not living within cities or metropolitan centers, was still about half. It would be safe to say, therefore, that anyone alive today who is more than fifty years old probably has a memory of either going hunting or watching some other family members, neighbor or friend going off with a gun into the woods.

This memory of a rural, small-town America which is bound up in hunting for game and sport, is a wonderful, nostalgic and romantic vision of what America used to be, but for people born thirty years ago or less, which is rapidly becoming more than half the total population, it's a vision to which they have no personal connection or memory whatsoever. The United States is rapidly becoming an overwhelmingly urbanized and cosmopolitan society, and within that type of environment hunters and hunting simply don't fit. To the extent that there are still nearly 60 million people living in non-urban or non-suburban zones, the flight of younger people away from these areas means that the population left behind gets relatively older all the time and the replenishment rate of such communities, and the hunting population within those communities will continue to decline.

In 2011 the U.S. Census reported that, for the first time in thirty years, there had been a slight uptick in the number of people who went to the outdoors to hunt birds and game, an increase over the previous five years of 9 percent. Yet despite the claims by NRA, NSSF and most of the national hunting organizations that this represented the beginnings of a true 'revival' of America returning to its past glories and historical roots, the evidence as yet doesn't really support the idea that hunting has once again become a part of the mainstream of American life. In fact, given the growth of the national population as a whole, the per capita increase in hunting was basically nil. More disquieting is the degree to which the proportion of the population in parts of the country traditionally strong in hunting increased by almost a negligible amount. Compare the two maps:

2006 pct. of hunting population by region

2011 pct. of hunting population by region.

Traditionally, hunting was always strongest in the South Atlantic, East and West South Central, East and West North Central and the Mountain regions. Of these six regions, the percentage of the population that hunted increased from 2006 to 2011 in only two – East South Central and

West North Central, and in neither region was the increase more than 2 percent. So while the numbers show a slight overall increase, one would certainly be hard-pressed to make the claim that this trend is substantial enough to show that America is once again adopting hunting as a mainstream sport. Furthermore, if the numbers don't show a strong movement back to hunting as a hobby and leisure sport, there is other data about who hunts and doesn't hunt that casts even more doubt on whether this small numerical revival means anything positive at all.

According to the National Shooting Sports Foundation, nearly 90% of all hunters pursue the sport within their own state of residence, and the data which I will now analyze covers only in-state hunts. To begin, slightly more than one-third of hunters go hunting for at least five consecutive years, but almost as many hunt only once every five years. Obviously the hunters who go out every year are more likely to continue hunting than those who don't, but the percentage of what we might call dedicated hunters isn't much greater than the percentage of what we might call casual hunters. If we add the hunters who go out two years out of five, the number climbs to 40% and three out of five years brings us to 60%. In other words, hunting is no longer a continuous or dedicated activity anywhere in the United States.

The next piece of bad news concerns the aging of the hunting population. The average age of hunters ranges from a low of 41 in the South, Midwest and West, to 45 in the Northeast. But since 2005 the average age has increased by nearly a half year in almost every region, and no region has seen a decline in the average age of all hunters, meaning that younger people are not replenishing the hunting population as the older generation naturally fades away. And while the average age continues to increase, the average income has at best remained steady or fallen behind. Of the 17 states that the NSSF tallied in their hunting survey, only one state – Oregon – reported that the median household income for hunters was more than 5% higher than the national median household income, while hunters in 8 other states had incomes equal to the national media but hunters in the other 8 states were at or below the national median.

Another problematic statistic regarding the health of hunting involves the percentage of hunters who live in rural, suburban or urban environments. Nationally, 53% of hunters live in rural areas, a number that is highest in the Southeast at 65% and lowest in the Northeast at

46%. But overall the rural population now counts for less than one in five, and in the Northeast and the West the percentage of rural dwellers is lower still. So while the country as a whole continues to see growth in urban and suburban zones, hunting as an activity lags behind in those areas and is strongest in the demographic environment that continues to lag behind. Hunting is also strongest in the occupational category that is eroding, namely, factory ad jobs in small towns. Nationally, the percentage of hunters in these two categories is 40%, rising to 56% in the Southeast and dropping to 35% in the West, largely reflecting the lack of small towns in the far western United States. And above all, no matter what category or region of the country we examine, the overwhelming majority of hunters, more than 80%, are male and white.

What is most striking about the data on who goes hunting is not the fact that there has been a slight uptick in numbers of hunters over the last several years. Rather, it is the degree to which the social and demographic profiles of the hunting population run counter to the evolving social and demographic profile of the country as a whole. It may take less than another two decades for a majority of the country's population to become non-white; it will probably take about the same amount of time for the percentage of the national population living in rural areas to dip under 10%. It should therefore come as no surprise that the NRA would shift its main focus away from hunting to protection from crime and the use of guns for self-defense. Roosevelt, Grinnell and other hunters started the conservation movement because they had every good reason to be worried about the disappearance of wild game. But how do you maintain an interest in conservation when it's the hunters, not the animals, who no longer can be found?

CHAPTER 6

DOES HUNTING HAVE A FUTURE?

Most people who are against hunting base their beliefs on the biblical maxim "Thou Shall Not Kill" and extend the injunction to all living things, not just to other human beings. This desire to preserve wildlife through hunting prohibitions is based partially on emotion (the animals are so lovable and cute) partially on ethics (killing anything is wrong) and partially on a prejudice about hunters based on differences in social class, status and lifestyles. In fact, it's a prejudice that cuts both ways, because just as the environmentalists consider hunters to be rough, uneducated louts sitting around drinking beer and chewing tobacco, so hunters believe the environmentalists to be those elitist, liberal tree-huggers who march around demanding civil rights for lesbians and gays.

Actually, there's an element of truth in both stereotypes, because you'll find an outdoor sports shop near every college campus, but in those stores 'outdoor sports' are defined as trekking, bird-watching and kayaking, whereas outlets that sell hunting and fishing, the traditional outdoor sporting activities, are rarely if ever found adjacent to college campuses or in college towns. And while the majority of active hunters come from households with at least average incomes, few of them have college educations or are members of the professional class. Meanwhile, college campuses have always been the primary recruiting-grounds for anything having to do with environmental action – the original Earth Day movement was born in college classrooms and its contemporary corollary, global warming, is promoted in unquestioned fashion in the standard curriculum of every university, often being introduced to students in as early as the ninth grade.

It would be misleading, however, if I were to write a book about hunting and environmentalism that only showed the differences between the two points of view. This is, unfortunately, the stance that is usually taken by advocates and advocacy groups on both sides, with the consequent loss both of understanding what the issues are really all about, along with a dilution of the political strength of both groups. So rather than coming together to find common ground and emphasize what hunters and environmentalists can agree on, most of their energies and resources are expended telling their followers why their opponents are wrong. Below is a picture that circulated far and wide showing Paul McCartney sitting next to a baby seal when he visited Canada in 2006 to protest the slaughter of baby seals:

Now how could anyone feel anything except a total and unquestioned desire to protect these lovable creatures from being clubbed to death for private financial gain? Except there's only one problem: all of the reliable studies on seal hunting indicate that the threat to seals from hunting is minimal compared to the threat from the disappearance of ice. Furthermore, the rate at which the sub-Arctic ice is melting, unless reversed, will nearly eradicate the entire seal population even if no hunting is allowed at all.

Yet the controversy over seal hunting, particularly the taking of younger, smaller seals by hitting them with clubs, continues with the hunters being labeled as "brutes" who practice "cruel" and "inhumane" ways of killing seals.

Meanwhile, the hunting and gun people are no less vitriolic in their condemnations of environmentalists whenever the latter organizations attempt to inject any part of their agenda into the debate about guns. The NRA, in particular, views any attempt to regulate or limit hunting as a back-door attack on gun ownership and routinely condemns any attempt to limit the magazine capacity of rifles as an effort to strip hunters of their 2nd Amendment rights to purchase or possess any type or style of rifle or accessory. But the most inflammatory rhetoric of the pro-gun community breaks out over the issue of assault rifles, or what the firearms industry now calls "modern sporting rifles." The campaign to promote military-style rifles as nothing more than a contemporary style updating of the traditional hunting rifle is a cynical attempt to create the impression that such weapons have a valid place in the arsenal of modern hunters, even when they come equipped with magazines that hold 30 rounds or more. The fact that hunting rifles chambered for center-fire calibers traditionally hold no more than five or six rounds, loads considered adequate by generations of hunters, is somehow ignored in the attempt to make mainstream America believe that an "assault rifle" is misnamed, misunderstood and therefore should not be subject to any regulation beyond the laws that cover other types of guns carried into the field.

Environmental organizations are not known for lining up explicitly against assault rifles, but a majority of their members tend to be in favor of gun control anyway and therefore usually side with advocacy groups like The Brady Campaign that seek to limit capacity and style of semi-automatic long guns. While the pro-gun lobby would like everyone to believe that the term "assault rifle" is a misnomer because it covers only fully-automatic guns (which isn't really true), the fact is that the gun industry began using the term "modern sporting rifle" to overcome resistance from family-oriented outdoor retail chains (Cabela's, Dick's, etc.) who refused to stock AR15-style weapons because they didn't want to risk offending consumers who walked into those stores to purchase kayaks, canoes, hiking gear or other items that appealed to the outdoor, non-hunting crowd.

Would it be a mistake to say that the communications gap between hunters and environmentalists is almost as great as the gap between pro-gun and anti-gun groups? Probably not, but perhaps it would be better to refer to it as a problem of understanding rather than communication. Because in the case of hunting, most of the argument on both sides revolves around the issue and existence of guns, rather than the impact and effect of hunting per se. This is because the United States is alone among all advanced countries to make little, if any distinction between ownership of hunting weapons, usually long guns like rifles and shotguns, as opposed to ownership of guns for personal defense; i.e., hand guns. In Canada, for example, the ownership of rifles and shotguns for sporting purposes has long been recognized and affirmed in law, but handguns are subject to universal registration and civilian ownership of handguns of less than 4 inches is prohibited altogether. And while there have been continued efforts to loosen the registration requirements even further, there has been little, if any public demand for the kind of free-wheeling acceptance of concealed-carry of handguns that has spread throughout the United States.

On the other hand, since there is no published study that breaks down American gun ownership on the basis of the kind of weapon that is owned, it is difficult to say with any certainty whether the same people who own handguns are the same people who own long guns, or vice-versa. One interesting trend which emerges most clearly in the annual gun poll conducted by the Gallup Organization shows that, over the last thirty years, while the percentage of households admitting to gun ownership has decreased, the percentage of respondents who claim that personal defense is their primary reason for owning a gun has increased. It's also the case that when the ATF began tracking gun manufacture by type of weapon in the 1970's, rifles and shotguns outnumbered handguns by a factor of two to one, whereas today if we eliminate military-style rifles from the overall number of rifles manufactured, the ratio of handguns to long guns coming onto the market has basically reversed. And these trends, more handguns than long guns and gun purchases primarily for personal defense, have taken place precisely over the period when the number of hunters has continued to decline.

So while we cannot necessarily say that the same households that used to contain rifles and shotguns have now switched to containing revolvers and pistols in addition to the long guns, there's no doubt that, generally speaking, gun owners still feel a kindred spirit with other gun owners, regardless of what types of guns are involved. And this is the reason why the NRA always weighs in on laws that might negatively impact hunters, such as the dispute over lead ammunition, because a threat to any kind of gun ownership is a threat to every kind of gun ownership. In case you've forgotten, that's what the 2nd Amendment's all about. And there isn't a gun owner out there who hasn't, in one way or another, been made to feel that the government, particularly the government as reflected by the current occupant of the White House, is an enemy of the 2nd Amendment.

Daniel Boone – old and new

Regrettably, since the degree to which gun ownership for the purposes of hunting has been identified as just another slice of the great gun debate, to be argued as noisily and nastily as every other aspect of the gun debate, so the role of hunting and hunters both in the past and present suffers from a lack of clarity and understanding on both sides. Which is what the remaining pages of this chapter and this book will try to explore. Because the truth is that even though much of our early folklore is comprised of fanciful and but somewhat realistic portraits of hunters and outdoorsmen like Jim Bridges and Daniel Boone, much of what they really represented in terms of America's relationship to its frontier has disappeared from the dialog and, in fact, began to be lost almost from the time that these explorers and hunters entered the wilderness itself.

To set this discussion in its proper context, what's important to remember above all is how quickly the American frontier, and behind the frontier its wilderness, disappeared. Let's spend a moment, for example, reviewing the life of Daniel Boone. Born in 1734, he is credited with having discovered the Cumberland Gap which opened Kentucky to trade and settlement back to Virginia and Tennessee. By blazing a route of settlement through the Appalachians, Boone effectively opened the first great stretch of wilderness to populations that had, previous to that date, been largely located along the Eastern coast. In 1784 he published a book of his exploits in the wilderness which created the same kind of sensation in towns and cities throughout the newly-emerging United States that Marco Polo's descriptions of his travels to China provoked in Italy when he returned from the Court of the Kublai Khan.

When the first national census was conducted in 1790, six years after the appearance of Boone's book, the population center of the country (the point midway between the furthest known location of American citizens) was placed at the point just below the confluence of the Delaware river and the Chesapeake Bay. In 1830, the year of Boone's death, the population center of the country had moved west to a point on the border of Virginia and West Virginia that was adjacent to the Harper's Ferry arsenal attacked in 1859. At the beginning of the Civil War, the central point of the country's settlement was moved to the middle of Ohio and by 1890, when Roosevelt was galloping around and writing his stories about hunting on the frontier, the Bureau of the Census declared that the frontier was entirely closed.

The photo above was taken in 1910, and the gentleman in the picture was standing about midway across Indiana. Could he have been alive the year that Daniel Boone died? Probably not, but his father probably was. Could he have read in a newspaper about Custer's Last Stand? Probably yes. Was he alive when the frontier officially came to an end? Of course. He also probably owned mechanized farm machinery, and his harvest was shipped to commercial granaries and thence to food processors in Chicago or other points East and West. He may have been a visitor to the Great Fair in Chicago and he may have already bought his first car.

That's how quickly the American frontier was settled and the wilderness came to an end. If you were alive the day that George Washington issued the first Presidential Thanksgiving Proclamation in 1789 you were probably alive when Daniel Boone went through the Cumberland and opened the first Western frontier. Which is a story you could have heard from your father or mother who read Boone's book that you then read as you bumped along in a train going from San Francisco to New York. It wasn't just the fact that we penetrated, subdued and closed our wilderness so quickly that makes our country's development so unique. It's the fact that our collective memory and consciousness of that process also was shaped by the extraordinary degree of modernization and industrial progress that took place at the same time.

Precisely because the penetration and subjugation of our wilderness (and the indigenous peoples encountered therein) occurred at such a rapid pace alongside an equally-rapid industrialization, Americans were able almost immediately to fashion a version of what had existed beyond the frontier that corresponded much more with what they wanted the frontier to represent than what in reality had actually existed before wilderness came to an end. And what was uppermost in the minds of conservationists who created this post-wilderness portrait was a nostalgic view of wilderness that, according to William Cronon, would contrast with the "debilitating effects" of urban-industrial life. Even though many of these self-same conservationists, like Roosevelt and Grinnell, represented an upper-class elite whose wealth and status grew out of industry, commerce and trade, they nevertheless felt themselves to be the custodians of a wilderness legacy that they only experienced after an earlier generation of rough-hewn explorers and hunters paved the way.

For the truth is that the wilderness may have been the place where Roosevelt learned the skills and aptitudes that transformed this sickly rube from back east into a man whose prowess would propel him to achieve the highest level of prominence in the land. But for most wilderness settlers, the ones who chose to go out into remote areas, clear land, plant crops, husband some animals and wait for the region around them to become a settled and developed zone, the wilderness was a harsh and largely unyielding place. Even Roosevelt discovered the dangers of wilderness existence by dint of losing almost his entire cattle herd because of a scorching summer followed by severe winter blizzards in 1886. And while his ranch collapsed and the nearby town of Medora quickly disappeared, at least Roosevelt had the wherewithal to return to the East and continue his socially respectable life. That certainly would not have been the case had he been a typical frontier settler who journeyed from an urban metropolis in a horse-drawn wagon followed by a mule.

So while the settlers who went out to the frontier did their utmost to clear the wilderness and thus protect themselves from the dangers of undeveloped and unsettled space, the ones who stayed behind in the urban centers very quickly lost any contact or awareness of wilderness because of the commoditization of products that were coming out of the wilderness zone. Whether it was breakfast cereals whose manufacture was centered around Battle Creek, Michigan and started appearing as early as the 1870s, or processed meats that were shipped in refrigerated railroad cars at about the same date, products from what had been the Western frontier in the 1830s could get to New York in three days or less by the time the Census said in 1890 that the frontier was now closed.

Perhaps it would clarify things if we were to substitute the word modernization for the word industrialization. Because the latter evokes images of the transformation from hand production to mass production on machines, whereas the social and economic changes that took place in America while the Western frontier was being closed went far beyond just the issue of how things were produced. For one thing, the period saw the rapid growth of cities and a general urbanization of everyday life; communication, transportation, education, all of these things changed in unprecedented ways during the second half of the nineteenth century. And these changes, even if they were felt first and were most pronounced in the larger cities, flowed back to the smaller towns and the countryside, in the same way that goods manufactured from raw materials brought to the urban marketplace from the frontier then were returned to country dwellers in the form of finished consumer goods, which even the most isolated rural settlers could now purchase for their homes.

What this meant was that the process of opening and exploiting the wilderness also meant becoming disconnected from the wilderness, the gradual replacement of all hand-made and hand-raised goods by mass-produced consumer articles which even found a market in the countryside villages and small towns. The urban dweller who sat down and ate his shredded wheat in the morning had no idea that this product may have been a live plant that had recently been harvested on a farm. By the same token, the farmer who ate the same bowl of cereal for breakfast might still have been able to look out his window and see a field of wheat, but he didn't take a few stalks into his barn to grind them into flour which then could be baked into bread. Chances are that his wife now purchased her flour in a general store that stocked a whole wall of wheat and rye-based products produced by a company called General Mills.

The commoditization of food also meant that hunting was no longer part of the natural cycle of birth, death and replacement of living things that defined wilderness and, for that matter, all existence. For hunters were now, like Kit Carson, either procurers of wilderness resources that could be turned into marketable products, such as furs, or like Teddy Roosevelt who hunted for sport. And to the degree that both types of hunting were no longer part of the natural cycle, these activities needed to be managed to insure that wildlife would not disappear as the natural balance between life and death was replaced by replenishment through artificial means. The wilderness eco-system that evolved and was always evolving in its natural state could not and did not survive once we began to exploit its resources for purposes having nothing to do with the existence of wilderness itself. The history of this wilderness exploitation began the moment that hunters began to kill game for reasons beyond feeding themselves.

Roosevelt and other early conservationists were clearly aware of this problem, and they tried to balance the requirements of environmental stewardship with the needs and demands of industrial development. And to a greater or lesser extent, the modern hunter-conservation movement remains remarkably aligned with the initial tenets of conservation behavior as first enunciated by Boone & Crockett and the other conservation groups. First and most important is the financial support for hunting that is derived from excise taxes on guns and ammunition, a special tax that flows through to conservation programs collected since 1937. All told, these tax revenues amounted to more than $370 million in 2011 and, according to the NSSF, these revenues along with all other expenditures related to hunting have increased by more than 50% over the last six years. In fact, following from the NSSF's report, Hunting in America, the total value of all hunting expenditures in 2011 - more than 38 billion – outpaced the revenues of both Google and Goldman Sachs.

It would be nice to imagine that something as traditional as hunting could create more value for the U.S. economy than the leading companies in financial services and IT, but the manner in which the NSSF derives those impressive numbers simply doesn't accord with the facts, indeed, not even with the facts presented by the NSSF. For example, the excise tax number is based on the sales of all ammunition and firearms, and it is impossible to break out with any degree of accuracy what proportion of those sales were the result of hunters purchasing guns or ammunition only to be used for a hunt. Since the expenditures for hunting equipment, travel and everything else purchased by hunters are based on samples which result in estimates at best, we really can't even tell to what degree these numbers reflect actual expenditures for things which may have had little or nothing to do with hunting at all. For example, according to the NSSF hunters spent more than

$150 million on bass and other boats, but I don't know a single state that allows shooting at animals from anywhere except on land. Perhaps every one of these boats was only used to transport hunters to their favorite location which could only be accessed by getting in and then out of a boat. Let's face it, that's a stretch.

But I don't want to belabor or nit-pick this data too much, because the fact is that hunters are really the only hobbyists whose purchase of the main items needed for the hunt – guns and ammo – requires the payment of a specific tax whether or not the hunters then go on to actually engage in their hobby or not. And if they choose to actually go hunting, they then must pay additional fees in the form of hunting licenses in order to engage in the sport. Other than sales taxes which are paid when any hobbyist, including hunters, must pay when they purchase an item for their use, I don't believe that model train hobbyists are subject to any additional levies in order to run those little engines and cars around on a track in the playroom or the garage. But people who play with model trains don't run them over land that belongs to anyone other than themselves. The whole point about hunting is that it's pretty tough to engage in the sport unless you go into the habitat where the game actually lives. And it is the issue of habitat, how it's defined and how it's protected that brings us to the real challenge between hunter-conservationists versus environmentalists that we face today.

Let's first look at habitat from the hunter's perspective. The approach that is most frequently cited is something called The North American Model of Wildlife Conservation. This doctrine, an outgrowth of the "fair chase" model of Roosevelt and Boone & Crockett, sees wildlife management as a cooperative effort between enlightened hunters and government agencies working together to preserve wildlife species through protection of habitat. But the notion of habitat, once considered to be only those areas specifically set aside for wildlife protection such as government or private game preserves, is now extended to cover all areas where wildlife may be found to exist, and the principles of wildlife management in the North American Model applies equally to all those places.

This idea of a wildlife management system applicable to all natural areas and all species was the handiwork of Aldo Leopold, another elite Easterner who went west to work for the Forest Service after completing his graduate study in forestry at Yale. Eventually, Leopold ended up as the first game management professor in the United States, receiving an appointment in 1933 as a Professor of Game Management at the University of Wisconsin where he remained until he suffered an untimely heart attack and died in 1948. While at Wisconsin, Leopold began to develop his theories about game management and also wrote a book, A Sand County Almanac, which became a best-selling work on conservation in the decades following his death.

Leopold's approach to conservation is most clearly set out in the North American Model updated and published on a regular basis by The Wildlife Society and Boone & Crockett Club, the two organizations that consciously link their approach back to the legacy of Roosevelt and the other early hunter-conservationists. The North American model consists of seven components or what are referred to as "principles" of wildlife management, which should be followed in all environments, regardless of whether the regions in question are under the control of public or private hands. These principles are what hunters and conservationists should strive to implement in any place where humans and wildlife need to co-exist, and can be summed up as follows: (1)

All wildlife is a public trust (meaning it needs to be preserved); (2) commercial taking of game (poaching, night-hunting) is forbidden; (3) wildlife access is by law–permits, fees, seasons, quotas; (4) killing only for 'legitimate' purposes, or the Rooseveltian notion of a 'fair' hunt; (5) wildlife is an international resource–treaties and cooperative agreements between countries that share common migrations of animals, fish and birds; (6) wildlife policy is based on scientific study, the major contribution of Leopold and his followers; (7) democratic access to wildlife is required–social class, status or wealth does not determine who shall hunt or where they can hunt.

The North American Model of Wildlife Conservation is supported by virtually every hunting organization (Ducks Unlimited, Rocky Mountain Elk Foundation, National Wild Turkey Federation, etc.), along with the gun advocacy groups like the NRA and NSSF. In particular, the latter groups can always be counted on to trot out their support for democratic hunting, because this principle folds in nicely to their endless campaigns to "defend" the 2nd Amendment on behalf of the common folks. But the Wildlife Society, which sees itself as the steward of the North American Model, is not quite as committed to the 2nd Amendment as the gun organizations would lead one to believe, because the Model in its latest Wildlife Society iteration calls only for supporting "commerce in sporting firearms and ammunition," which can be read along fairly narrow lines. In addition, the Wildlife Society in 2009 took a formal, negative position on the question of lead ammunition, and while its leadership council called for a phased-in and "collaborative" approach to banning lead-based ammunition components from all hunting activities, their opposition to lead ammunition and their support of educational efforts to "promote greater public awareness of the consequences of lead exposure to wildlife populations" makes it clear that on this question they side with Audubon and not the NRA.

Uppermost in the minds of supporters of the North American Model, however, seems to be a concern for how to support the financial costs of habitat conservation, given the fact that between sixty and ninety percent of state wildlife budgets are derived from licensing fees and levies collected from the people who actually engage in the hunt. And notwithstanding the recent uptick in gun sales, hunting licenses and other related revenues, the fact is that the general downward trend in hunting activity means a downward trend in conservation spending as well. The NSSF was quick to point out recently that hunting had increased between 2006 and 2011 by 9%, while the number of people journeying away from their home areas to view wildlife (i.e. the tree hugging people) declined during the same period by 4%, but the truth is that the financial benefits derived from expenditures for hunting is but a fraction of the financial returns generated by the more than 80 million Americans, 16 years or older, who reported that they visited either nearby or faraway locations to view wildlife or otherwise immerse themselves in a nature experience.

While the data on both hunting and tree-hugging is still not specific enough to tell us anything about the spending habits of these two populations except in the most general terms, a quick perusal of state wildlife regulations makes it clear that, at least for the specific costs of access to wildlife, the hunting folks are getting off cheap. The average cost of a season-long big game hunting license for state residents in all the 50 states seems to be somewhat less than fifty dollars, while senior hunters pay as little as ten bucks and in some states hunt for free. License fees for non-residents are substantially higher, in particular states that attract hunters from faraway locations in order to go after the most exotic big species like bear and elk. But this population constitutes only a fraction, at most 10% of the hunters who go out to the woods and flyways in just about every state. Meanwhile, it is not unusual for a state park to charge ten or more dollars per day for every car that comes into the park, and a family of four will probably have to pay $100 for a day's admission to the local zoo. Even the financial burden that hunters face from excise taxes on guns and ammo is something of an illusion, because guns aren't expendable and certainly most hunters are using the same gun they used the year before. And while premium hunting ammunition has lately risen in price thanks to fanciful theories about how Obama is buying up all the ammo in a back-door strategy to disarm America, most hunters can get through an entire season without using up more than one box.

For all the talk about how much money hunters generate for habitat conservation, the fact is that on the scale of most outdoor sporting activities, hunters get to engage in their hobby at a bargain-basement price. Which is fine, when you stop to think about it, given the fact that hunting is still primarily a working-class and blue-collar sport. But this still doesn't answer the real problem of habitat preservation, given the thinning and graying of the hunting population, particularly in rural areas where a majority of American hunters live.

Which brings us to the other side of the coin, namely, the issue of habitat preservation on the part of the majority of Americans who also enjoy nature and the outdoors, but in more and more parts of the country do not engage in the hunt. At the same time, the ultimate goal of both hunters and non-hunting nature lovers, as Irena Knezevic and others have pointed out, are not necessarily in conflict with one another, because both groups want to protect wildlife, manage natural resources and re-connect people to nature and the natural environment. The difference, however, which is what turned non-hunting conservationists into environmentalists, is that the latter view habitat as embracing all living species, including humans, and feel the management of resources must be accomplished in a way that favors nature and natural environments over commercial and industrial development. And it is over the question of management balance between habitat on the one hand and industrialization on the other that the conflict between hunter-conservationists and environmentalists is most intense.

By definition, the search for and exploitation of extractive resources poses a threat to nature and therefore a threat to natural habitat. And given the technologies that are available today for resource exploitation, along with the increasing demand for such resources, ultimately government becomes the arbiter of how much of the habitat will be consigned to natural preservation, as opposed to how much will be opened for industrial and extractive exploitation. But the problem is more complicated because the same science that, following the North American Model, can be used to manage habitat, is also the same science that increasingly rejects the notion that one can create, as it were, artificial boundaries between habitat that will be preserved and habitat that will be exploited. If you don't believe me, just tune into the evening news where you'll always see or hear yet another story about the Keystone Pipeline, or Alaska's North Slope or some other place that's become the latest hot-button spot for the debate about global warming. Remember "Drill baby, drill"?

It is impossible nowadays to detach the argument over habitat preservation from the argument over the role of government, given the degree to which government plays a central role in both. And if you're a gun owner and a hunter, chances are you favor less government activity in all things, particularly anything related to guns; while if you're an environmentalist, you're also someone who generally believes that government needs to be as aggressive as possible in controlling what would otherwise become an environment completely at the mercy of the excesses of industrial and economic growth. And this division is not only true in terms of the arguments over habitat and environment, it has a long legacy that is evident in other areas as well. Remember that the region of the United States whose communities contain the largest proportion of hunters is the Old South, with states like Mississippi, Alabama and Georgia being the only states in the entire USA where the proportion of hunters within the statewide population is twice the proportion of hunters in the country as a whole. Meanwhile, where do a majority of the tree huggers and wildlife watchers live? North of the Mason-Dixon line; where else?

So the argument between hunting and environmentalism, like virtually every argument between gun owners and non-gun owners, breaks down along geographic and therefore cultural lines. And don't think for one second that it's only the good ol' boys down yonder who are passionate in their beliefs. Take, for example, a recent increase in the number of people in northern West Coast locations around Vancouver and Seattle who have decided to "get into" hunting as a way of consuming only "wild" game meat. Some of these people call themselves "recovering vegetarians," others see hunting and consuming free-ranging animals as a way of sustaining both themselves and the species that they eat. Still others go beyond this belief and take hunting lessons from native Americans and Eskimos whom they know to be the only people who understand and practice bio-diversity methods that work. Of course we can ignore the numerous scientific studies conducted by the National Wildlife Health Center, a division of the United States Geological Survey, which lists the numerous toxins and parasites that people might ingest from consuming this so-called 'pure' meat. What do those scientists know? After all, according to one natural hunter and meat consumer in Vancouver, the whole point of this activity is to "minimize both nutritional and ethical evil." Try arguing with that defender of wildlife.

It's unfortunate that gun ownership has become such a politicized issue that the two sides lose sight of the fact that when it comes to habit and environment, they actually share the same goals. And if a way could be found to set aside some of the more emotional rhetoric and close down some of the louder proponents of that rhetoric, perhaps a lot more could get done. Because what the NRA goes out of its way to avoid telling its members is that the only thing that's standing between them and a successful takeaway of their guns was the ability of a few state Republican parties to gerrymander the 2010 election results that gave Red majorities to some Congressional delegations even where they collected a minority of the votes. As for the many environmentalists who can usually be counted on to support gun control, they might remember that making it more difficult for law-abiding hunters to keep their guns means a more rapid decline in the size of a population whose passion for their hobby is what pays the costs of preserving the trees that the environmentalists love to hug. You would think that such rational arguments might allow hunters and environmentalists to find common ground. We seem to live at a time, however, when common ground is the last thing we want to find.

I like to end my books with a personal anecdote, so here goes. A couple of years ago I was contacted by a guy who lived in a house on the edge of town. His back yard faced some pretty deep woods. And one morning as he was standing in his kitchen making coffee he looked out the window and sitting on his back deck was a pretty good-sized black bear. So he right away put down the coffee, picked up the telephone and called the Fish and Game people to come and get rid of the bear. Only he was told that unless the bear had actually attacked someone or someone's pet, it was not considered a threat and therefore could not be removed – at least not by them.

At which point he called me in my gun shop and asked if I could come by with a rifle or a shotgun and shoot the bear. But the problem, as I told him, was that bears were protected in Massachusetts, which means they couldn't be hunted or shot, so there was nothing I could do. But then I suggested to him that if he had a portable radio he could stick it in the open window, turn the volume up as high as it would go and the noise would probably scare the bear away. So the man put down the phone, went into the bedroom, yanked the radio out of the wall and came back into the kitchen to plug it in and play the music as loud as he could. Except that when he came back into the kitchen and looked out on his deck, the bear was gone.

* * *

Notes for Further Reading and Notes About Everything Else

I have tried to cite most of the books I used for reference in the chapter texts, but sometimes I missed. Either way what follows is a not-exhaustive list of sources, but if you read any or all of these works you'll enjoy them because they really are books of distinction and scholarly eminence. If there was one thing I liked about writing this volume, it was the fact that I went back and re-read or read for the first time books that everyone should read. They are all that good.

Chapter 1

The best book, in my opinion, on the Indian Wars is, Thomas Powers, *The Killing of Crazy Horse*. The author doesn't miss anything.

Another not-to-miss work is, John D. McDermott, *A Guide to the Indian Wars of the West*.

A classic: Roderick Frazier Nash, *Wilderness and the American Mind*.

Valuable excerpts from the Lewis & Clark expedition and others: John Bakeless, *America as Seen by its First Explorers.*

Memoirs and diaries of early hunters are from a collection housed (and online) at the remarkable Museum of the Mountain Man in Wyoming whose book *The Fur Trade and Rendezvous of the Green River Valley* was also a valuable resource. I am indebted to Jim Hardee of the Museum's staff for his efforts and help in securing resources for me to use.

Some valuable portraits of Indian life are also found in Francis Parkman, *The Oregon Trail.*

To a greater or lesser extent the "Turner thesis" has been updated and revised by a new generation of western historians, chief among them being Patricia Nelson Limerick, *The Legacy of Conquest, The Unbroken Past of the American West.*

Susan Sleeper-Smith, *Rethinking the Fur Trade, Cultures of Exchange in an Atlantic World.* Unfortunately almost all of the articles in this remarkable collection cover a chronology (16th - 18th Centuries) that is largely outside the scope of my book. But it's interesting to note that from the beginning of the pelts/finished goods exchange between Indians and Europeans, the Indians often refused to deliver beaver furs because they felt they were receiving finished goods, mostly clothing, of inferior quality. So much for the notion that whites were dealing with less-civilized people.

Chapter 2

I'm not exactly sure how he was able to distill the essence of Roosevelt's conservationist contribution from the veritable avalanche of words written by and about our 26th President, but he did and in this respect Douglas Brinkley's *The Wilderness Warrior, Theodore Roosevelt and the Crusade for America* must rank as one of the leading works of American history of this or any other time.

Close behind Brinkley in terms of its value to my book is the work of my former graduate-school chum and classmate, John Reiger, *American Sportsmen and the Origins of Conservation.* What Brinkley did for Roosevelt, Reiger has done for Grinnell in *The Passing of the West, Selected Papers of George Bird Grinnell.*

Carl P Russell's, *Guns on the Early Frontiers* is a lot more than just about guns and deserves mention and attention in any work about the American West.

Chapter 3

Much of the data for Chapter 3 can be found in the online repository for the U.S. Census stored on a website administered by the University of Minnesota. Better than the data itself is a fairly good search engine that allows one to compare and contrast data from the various censuses beginning with the first census in 1790.

I was oriented about the ecological role of beavers by reading research published online by Toby Hemenway, in particular from his website http://www.patternliteracy.com/.

Saving this book for last, you think you know a lot and then you read a book and realize that you don't know much at all. Want to play that game? Read William Cronon, *Nature's Metropolis, Chicago and the Great West*. His essays in *Uncommon Ground: Rethinking the Human Place in Nature*, will also make you feel very modest about how much you really know about anything.

Chapter 4

A good place to start thinking about Carson is the website (http://www.rachelcarson.org/) devoted to her life and works.

The best book about the 60's and the counterculture that followed is Hunter Thompson's The Great Shark Hunt, Strange

Tales from a Strange Time. You would think that someone would have come up with the bright idea to publish a collection of his Rolling Stone stories from the 60s, but I don't believe that any such collection exists. And I still can't find any reference on the internet to the recipe for Empress Chili which appeared in the only issue of Rolling Stone to ever sell out. Anyone who has this recipe can send it to me at mike@mikethegunguy.com.

Chapter 5

Traditional hunting practices in England are covered by Edward P. Thompson, Whigs and Hunters and Douglas Hay, et. al., *Albion's Fatal Tree.*

The data for this chapter comes from two published sources, which are the NSSF's *A Portrait of Hunters and Hunting License National Trends,* and the U.S. Fish and Wildlife Service *National Survey of Fishing, Hunting and Wildlife-Associated Recreation.*

Chapter 6

The North American Model of Wildlife Conservation is regularly published and updated by The Wildlife Society.

Interesting approaches to conservation and environment can be found in Human Dimensions of Wildlife: An International Journal, from which I quote the article by Irena Knezevic.

ABOUT THE AUTHOR

Michael R. Weisser was born in Washington, D.C., educated in New York City public schools and received a Ph.D. in Economic History at Northwestern University. He is a featured blogger with Huffington Post and also blogs about guns at www.mikethegunguy.com. Since 1978 he has been a firearms retailer, wholesaler, law enforcement distributor and importer with total gun sales in excess of 30,000 handguns, rifles and shotguns. He is also a Life Member of the NRA and a certified firearms instructor in six specialties. He can be reached at his blog or at mike@mikethegunguy.com.